MAX LUCADO

LIFE LESSONS *from*

COLOSSIANS & PHILEMON

The Difference Christ Makes

PREPARED BY THE LIVINGSTONE CORPORATION

THOMAS NELSON
Since 1798

Life Lessons from Colossians and Philemon

© 2018 by Max Lucado

Published in Nashville, Tennessee, by Thomas Nelson. Thomas Nelson is a registered trademark of HarperCollins Christian Publishing, Inc.

Produced with the assistance of the Livingstone Corporation. Project staff include Jake Barton, Joel Bartlett, Andy Culbertson, Mary Horner Collins, Will Reaves, and Rachel Hawkins.

Editor: Len Woods

All Scripture quotations, unless otherwise indicated, are taken from The Holy Bible, New International Version®, NIV®. Copyright © 1973, 1978, 1984, 2011 by Biblica, Inc.™ Used by permission. All rights reserved worldwide.

Scripture quotations marked MSG are taken from THE MESSAGE. Copyright © 1993, 1994, 1995, 1996, 2000, 2001, 2002. Used by permission of NavPress Publishing Group.

Scripture quotations marked NCV are taken from the New Century Version®. Copyright © 1987, 1988, 1991 by Word Publishing. All rights reserved.

Scripture quotations marked NKJV are taken from the New King James Version®. Copyright © 1982 by Thomas Nelson. Used by permission. All rights reserved.

Scripture quotations marked NASB are taken from The NEW AMERICAN STANDARD BIBLE®, Copyright © 1960, 1962, 1963, 1968, 1971, 1972, 1973, 1975, 1977, 1995 by The Lockman Foundation. Used by permission.

Material for the "Inspiration" sections taken from the following books:

And the Angels Were Silent. Copyright © 1992, 2004 by Max Lucado. Thomas Nelson, a registered trademark of HarperCollins Christian Publishing, Inc., Nashville, Tennessee.

Anxious for Nothing. Copyright © 2017 by Max Lucado. Thomas Nelson, a registered trademark of HarperCollins Christian Publishing, Inc., Nashville, Tennessee.

The Applause of Heaven. Copyright © 1990, 1996, 1999 by Max Lucado. Thomas Nelson, a registered trademark of HarperCollins Christian Publishing, Inc., Nashville, Tennessee.

Come Thirsty. Copyright © 2004 by Max Lucado. Thomas Nelson, a registered trademark of HarperCollins Christian Publishing, Inc., Nashville, Tennessee.

Cure for the Common Life. Copyright © 2005 by Max Lucado. Thomas Nelson, a registered trademark of HarperCollins Christian Publishing, Inc., Nashville, Tennessee.

A Gentle Thunder. Copyright © 1995 by Max Lucado. Thomas Nelson, a registered trademark of HarperCollins Christian Publishing, Inc., Nashville, Tennessee.

God Came Near. Copyright © 2004 by Max Lucado. Thomas Nelson, a registered trademark of HarperCollins Christian Publishing, Inc., Nashville, Tennessee.

The Great House of God. Copyright © 1997 by Max Lucado. Thomas Nelson, a registered trademark of HarperCollins Christian Publishing, Inc., Nashville, Tennessee.

It's Not About Me. Copyright © 2004 by Max Lucado. Thomas Nelson, a registered trademark of HarperCollins Christian Publishing, Inc., Nashville, Tennessee.

A Love Worth Giving. Copyright © 2002 by Max Lucado. Thomas Nelson, a registered trademark of HarperCollins Christian Publishing, Inc., Nashville, Tennessee.

Next Door Savior. Copyright © 2003 by Max Lucado. Thomas Nelson, a registered trademark of HarperCollins Christian Publishing, Inc., Nashville, Tennessee.

Six Hours One Friday. Copyright © 2004 by Max Lucado. Thomas Nelson, a registered trademark of HarperCollins Christian Publishing, Inc., Nashville, Tennessee.

Thomas Nelson titles may be purchased in bulk for educational, business, fundraising, or sales promotional use. For information, please e-mail SpecialMarkets@ThomasNelson.com.

ISBN 978-0-310-08652-9

First Printing May 2018 / Printed in the United States of America

CONTENTS

HOW TO STUDY THE BIBLE

The Bible is a peculiar book. Words crafted in another language. Deeds done in a distant era. Events recorded in a far-off land. Counsel offered to a foreign people. It is a peculiar book.

It's surprising that anyone reads it. It's too old. Some of its writings date back 5,000 years. It's too bizarre. The book speaks of incredible floods, fires, earthquakes, and people with supernatural abilities. It's too radical. The Bible calls for undying devotion to a carpenter who called himself God's Son.

Logic says this book shouldn't survive. Too old, too bizarre, too radical.

The Bible has been banned, burned, scoffed, and ridiculed. Scholars have mocked it as foolish. Kings have branded it as illegal. A thousand times over the grave has been dug and the dirge has begun, but somehow the Bible never stays in the grave. Not only has it survived, but it has also thrived. It is the single most popular book in all of history. It has been the bestselling book in the world for years!

There is no way on earth to explain it. Which perhaps is the only explanation. For the Bible's durability is not found on *earth* but in *heaven*. The millions who have tested its claims and claimed its promises know there is but one answer: the Bible is God's book and God's voice.

As you read it, you would be wise to give some thought to two questions: *What is the purpose of the Bible?* and *How do I study the Bible?* Time spent reflecting on these two issues will greatly enhance your Bible study.

What is the purpose of the Bible?

Let the Bible itself answer that question: *"From infancy you have known the Holy Scriptures, which are able to make you wise for salvation through faith in Christ Jesus"* (2 Timothy 3:15).

The purpose of the Bible? Salvation. God's highest passion is to get his children home. His book, the Bible, describes his plan of salvation. The purpose of the Bible is to proclaim God's plan and passion to save his children.

This is the reason why this book has endured through the centuries. It dares to tackle the toughest questions about life: *Where do I go after I die? Is there a God? What do I do with my fears?* The Bible is the treasure map that leads to God's highest treasure—eternal life.

But how do you study the Bible? Countless copies of Scripture sit unread on bookshelves and nightstands simply because people don't know how to read it. What can you do to make the Bible real in your life?

The clearest answer is found in the words of Jesus: *"Ask and it will be given to you; seek and you will find; knock and the door will be opened to you"* (Matthew 7:7).

The first step in understanding the Bible is asking God to help you. You should read it prayerfully. If anyone understands God's Word, it is because of God and not the reader.

"The Advocate, the Holy Spirit, whom the Father will send in my name, will teach you all things and will remind you of everything I have said to you" (John 14:26).

Before reading the Bible, pray and invite God to speak to you. Don't go to Scripture looking for your idea, but go searching for his.

Not only should you read the Bible prayerfully, but you should also read it carefully. *"Seek and you will find"* is the pledge. The Bible is not a newspaper to be skimmed but rather a mine to be quarried. *"If you look for it as for silver and search for it as for hidden treasure, then you will understand the fear of the LORD and find the knowledge of God"* (Proverbs 2:4–5).

Any worthy find requires effort. The Bible is no exception. To understand the Bible, you don't have to be brilliant, but you must be willing to roll up your sleeves and search.

"Do your best to present yourself to God as one approved, a worker who does not need to be ashamed and who correctly handles the word of truth" (2 Timothy 2:15).

Here's a practical point. Study the Bible a bit at a time. Hunger is not satisfied by eating twenty-one meals in one sitting once a week. The body needs a steady diet to remain strong. So does the soul. When God sent food to his people in the wilderness, he didn't provide loaves already made. Instead, he sent them manna in the shape of *"thin flakes like frost on the ground"* (Exodus 16:14).

God gave manna in limited portions.

God sends spiritual food the same way. He opens the heavens with just enough nutrients for today's hunger. He provides *"a rule for this, a rule for that; a little here, a little there"* (Isaiah 28:10).

Don't be discouraged if your reading reaps a small harvest. Some days a lesser portion is all that is needed. What is important is to search every day for that day's message. A steady diet of God's Word over a lifetime builds a healthy soul and mind.

It's much like the little girl who returned from her first day at school feeling a bit dejected. Her mom asked, "Did you learn anything?"

"Apparently not enough," the girl responded. "I have to go back tomorrow, and the next day, and the next . . . "

Such is the case with learning. And such is the case with Bible study. Understanding comes little by little over a lifetime.

There is a third step in understanding the Bible. After the asking and seeking comes the knocking. After you ask and search, *"knock and the door will be opened to you"* (Matthew 7:7).

To knock is to stand at God's door. To make yourself available. To climb the steps, cross the porch, stand at the doorway, and volunteer. Knocking goes beyond the realm of thinking and into the realm of acting.

To knock is to ask, *What can I do? How can I obey? Where can I go?*

It's one thing to know what to do. It's another to do it. But for those who do it—those who choose to obey—a special reward awaits them.

"Whoever looks intently into the perfect law that gives freedom, and continues in it—not forgetting what they have heard, but doing it—they will be blessed in what they do" (James 1:25).

What a promise. Blessings come to those who do what they read in God's Word! It's the same with medicine. If you only read the label but ignore the pills, it won't help. It's the same with food. If you only read the recipe but never cook, you won't be fed. And it's the same with the Bible. If you only read the words but never obey, you'll never know the joy God has promised.

Ask. Search. Knock. Simple, isn't it? So why don't you give it a try? If you do, you'll see why the Bible is the most remarkable book in history.

INTRODUCTION TO
The Books of Colossians and Philemon

COLOSSIANS

The renowned British author and theologian C.S. Lewis once noted that most Christians need reminding more than they need instruction. How insightful. How true.

We are a forgetful people. Sadly, when we lose sight of God's amazing promises to us, and his marvelous provisions for us, it is our all-too-common tendency to become proud.

We forget how desperate we were. We forget how merciful God has been. If we are not careful, we may begin to see salvation not as the toss of the life preserver to the drowning but as a journey in a row-boat: God's grace handling one oar and our noble efforts handling the other. It's not that Jesus isn't necessary; it's just that Jesus needs our assistance. We may even start imagining that God is lucky to have us on his team.

Slowly, subtly, we begin to embrace the doctrine of *salvation by Jesus plus*. Jesus plus good deeds. Jesus plus the right doctrine. Jesus plus the right Bible translation.

Or, in the case of the church in Colossae, Jesus plus the right religious feast, New Moon Festival, and Sabbath day. To the Christians in Colossae, the right rituals were every bit as important as the right Savior.

Paul would have none of this. He denounced the Jesus-plus philosophy as heretical. If we are saved, he insisted, it is only because God mercifully plucked us out of the deep and not because we scrambled into his boat, grabbed an oar, and started paddling.

Let the book of Colossians remind you of the great truth that Jesus is our all-in-all. He is all our souls need, and all our hearts desire. We become different and we make a difference by ordering our lives around the incomparable Christ.

AUTHOR AND DATE

Paul, who persecuted the early church before his life was radically altered by meeting the risen Jesus on the road to Damascus (see Acts 9:1–31). It appears the gospel first reached Colossae during the time Paul was ministering in Ephesus (see 19:1–10) through the efforts of his coworker Epaphras, who started a Christian assembly in the city. Paul most likely wrote Colossians c. AD 60 from Rome, where he was imprisoned at the time. Timothy, his fellow minister, might have been the scribe, and it was likely delivered by Tychicus and Onesimus (see Colossians 4:7–8), the latter of whom was the subject of Paul's letter to Philemon.

SITUATION

Although Paul was not the founder of the Colossian church, he presumably learned through Epaphras that though the congregation was thriving, a deceptive philosophy had taken root that could disrupt its stability. It appears that Paul's intent in writing the letter was thus more *proactive* than *reactive*, for he wanted to stamp out this false teaching before it could do damage. While the exact nature of these false doctrines is not known, it is clear from Paul's words that these teachings were seeking to devalue the work and supremacy of Christ.

KEY THEMES

- Faith, love, and hope are key to following Christ.
- In Christ Jesus, we have been offered freedom.
- Because of Jesus, Christians can be as in touch with the next world as this one.

KEY VERSE

Since, then, you have been raised with Christ, set your hearts on things above, where Christ is, seated at the right hand of God (Colossians 3:1).

CONTENTS

PHILEMON

Philemon had every reason to be angry. His slave, Onesimus, had stolen from him and run away. Somehow the thief made his way from Colossae to the city of Rome, where he *just happened* to meet the apostle Paul, who *just happened* to be an old friend of Philemon.

Transformed by the message of Christ, Onesimus, at Paul's request, is now returning to Philemon in Colossae. Under normal circumstances, Philemon has every right to exact revenge. But these are not normal circumstances. Onesimus fled as a slave; he returns as a believer and a spiritual brother. Paul doesn't ask Philemon to free Onesimus from slavery, but to free him from harsh vengeance. He urges Philemon to offer grace rather than demand justice.

Does this short letter have any application for your life? It does if there is an Onesimus in your world. It does if someone has betrayed you or offended you or turned away from you. Getting even would be the common desire. Demanding justice would be a natural response, which is precisely the problem. Christians aren't called to live naturally, but supernaturally.

As you consider how to respond to someone who has wronged you, consider Paul's exhortation to Philemon. Behind that, ponder the example of Christ. As his follower, your calling is to live by the higher law of God's kingdom, a law which sets all people, slave or non-slave, free.

That is the difference Christ makes.

AUTHOR AND DATE

Paul is believed to have written the short letter of Philemon either at the same time as Colossians (c. AD 60) or shortly before (c. AD 57). Paul states in both letters that he is a prisoner at the time of writing (see Colossians 4:10 and Philemon 1:1), but the fact that Paul asks Philemon to prepare a guest room for him (see verse 22) indicates he expected to be released and see the congregation in Colossae soon. Since Rome was 1,300 miles away, the more probable location of Paul's place of writing the letter is the city of Ephesus, and thus was likely composed at a different time from Colossians. Paul likely met Onesimus in Rome, and over time he became "useful" to the apostle (see verse 11). Philemon, the recipient of the letter, was evidently a close friend of Paul and lived in the city of Colossae.

SITUATION

Both Christians and non-Christians owned slaves in the Roman Empire. Onesimus, a slave from Colossae, had stolen from his owner, a man named Philemon, and run away. Paul likely met Onesimus while in prison in Rome, and there he led him to faith in Christ. Over time, Onesimus became "useful" to him—to the point that Paul could write he became his "son" while in chains (see verses 10–11). Paul was evidently a close friend of Philemon, so he wrote this letter asking for Philemon to forgive his runaway slave and accept him back without punishment.

KEY THEMES

- Salvation is not determined or affected by a person's station in life.
- The love God expects from us goes beyond the standards of this world.

KEY VERSES

Perhaps the reason he was separated from you for a little while was that you might have him back forever—no longer as a slave, but better than a slave, as a dear brother (verses 15–16).

CONTENTS

LESSON ONE

FAITH, HOPE, AND LOVE

We heard of your faith in Christ Jesus and of
your love for all the saints; because of the hope
which is laid up for you in heaven.
Colossians 1:4–5 nkjv

REFLECTION

Letter writing is quickly becoming a relic of a bygone era. With cell phones, email, and text messaging, few people sit down anymore with paper and pen, with the intent of composing a thoughtful correspondence. What are your own letter-writing habits?

_____

_____

_____

_____

_____

_____

_____

_____

_____

_____

_____

SITUATION

At some point during Paul's ministry—most likely during his imprisonment in Rome c. AD 60—the apostle learned the church in Colossae was being bombarded by an eclectic mix of heretical teachings. Although Paul did not found the church, he felt compelled to write a letter to them to guide them back to the true teachings of the gospel. His message to them was simply that Christ is preeminent. He is Creator and Lord—the all-sufficient Savior of the world. In our union with him—by grace and through faith—the Christian finds all he or she will ever need.

OBSERVATION

Read Colossians 1:1–8 from the New International
Version or the New King James Version.

NEW INTERNATIONAL VERSION

[1] Paul, an apostle of Christ Jesus by the will of God, and Timothy our brother,

[2] To God's holy people in Colossae, the faithful brothers and sisters in Christ:

Grace and peace to you from God our Father.

[3] We always thank God, the Father of our Lord Jesus Christ, when we pray for you, [4] because we have heard of your faith in Christ Jesus and of the love you have for all God's people—[5] the faith and love that spring from the hope stored up for you in heaven and about which you have already heard in the true message of the gospel [6] that has come to you. In the same way, the gospel is bearing fruit and growing throughout the whole world—just as it has been doing among you since the day you heard it and truly understood God's grace. [7] You learned it from Epaphras, our dear fellow servant, who is a faithful minister of Christ on our behalf, [8] and who also told us of your love in the Spirit.

NEW KING JAMES VERSION

[1] Paul, an apostle of Jesus Christ by the will of God, and Timothy our brother,

[2] To the saints and faithful brethren in Christ who are in Colosse:

Grace to you and peace from God our Father and the Lord Jesus Christ.

[3] We give thanks to the God and Father of our Lord Jesus Christ, praying always for you, [4] since we heard of your faith in Christ Jesus and of your love for all the saints; [5] because of the hope which is laid up for you in heaven, of which you heard before in the word of the truth of the gospel, [6] which has come to you, as it has also in all the world, and is

bringing forth fruit, as it is also among you since the day you heard and knew the grace of God in truth; [7] as you also learned from Epaphras, our dear fellow servant, who is a faithful minister of Christ on your behalf, [8] who also declared to us your love in the Spirit.

EXPLORATION

1. What do you learn about the Colossian believers from this brief introductory paragraph?

2. Why was Paul thankful for the Colossians?

3. What does Paul mean in this passage when he speaks of "hope"?

4. What is the connection between faith, hope, and love?

5. What do you remember most about the day when you "heard [the message of the gospel] and truly understood God's grace" (verse 6)?

6. How does Paul describe Epaphras? What role did he play in the Colossian church?

_____

_____

_____

INSPIRATION

Jesus said, "I am the bread that gives life. I am the light of the world. I am the resurrection and the life. . . . I am the door. I am the way, the truth, and the life. I will come back and take you with me." Jesus proclaiming— ever offering but never forcing.

Standing over the crippled man: "Do you want to get well?" (John 5:6).

Eye to eye with the blind man, now healed: "Do you believe in the Son of Man?" (9:35).

Near the tomb of Lazarus, probing the heart of Martha: "Whoever lives by believing in me will never die. Do you believe this?" (11:26).

Testing Pilate's motive: "Is that your own idea . . . or did others talk to you about me?" (18:34).

The first time John hears Jesus speak, Jesus asks a question, "What do you want?" (1:38). Among Jesus' last words is yet another: "Do you love me?" (21:17).

This is the Jesus whom John remembers. The honest questions. The thundering claims. The gentle touch. Never going where not invited, but once invited never stopping until he's finished, until a choice has been made.

God will whisper. He will shout. He will touch and tug. He will take away our burdens; he'll even take away our blessings. If there are a thousand steps between us and him, he will take all but one. But he will leave the final one for us. The choice is ours.

Please understand. His goal is not to make you happy. His goal is to make you his. His goal is not to get you what you want; it is to get you what you need. . . . Earthly discomfort is a glad swap for heavenly peace. Jesus said, "In this world you will have trouble. But take heart! I have overcome the world" (16:33). (From *A Gentle Thunder* by Max Lucado.)

REACTION

7. The Colossians heard the claims of Christ from Epaphras. Whom did God use to share the good news with you?

_____

_____

_____

8. Paul referred to his readers as "holy" (verse 2), a word that means being set apart or dedicated solely for God's use. What are the practical implications of this?

_____

_____

_____

9. What about your life would prompt your pastor, small-group leader, or mentor to feel thankful?

_____

_____

_____

10. How is the gospel bearing fruit and growing in your life?

_____

_____

_____

11. How can you tell if you are demonstrating "love in the Spirit" (verse 8)?

12. What does it mean to be "saints" (verse 2)?

LIFE LESSONS

Amazing things happen when we put our faith in Christ. We are born again (see John 3:3–8). We become God's children (see John 1:12–13). Our sins are forgiven (see Ephesians 1:7). We receive eternal life (see 1 John 5:11). God's Spirit takes up residence in our lives (see Romans 8:15). Not only do we enjoy all these blessings, but we also are infused with hope. Biblical hope is not a vague wish about the future; it is a sure and certain expectation. With that hope, we also receive a new capacity to love others. Faith, hope, and love. These are the defining marks of one who has experienced new life in Christ!

DEVOTION

Father in heaven, thank you for opening our eyes—and our hearts—to the truth of the gospel. Deepen our faith. Strengthen our hope. Increase our love. Cause the gospel to bear much fruit in and through our lives. We pray this in the great name of Christ.

JOURNALING

How does a deep and abiding hope in Christ lead to a life filled with love?

_____

_____

_____

_____

_____

_____

_____

_____

_____

_____

_____

_____

_____

_____

_____

_____

_____

_____

FOR FURTHER READING

To complete the books of Colossians and Philemon during this twelve-part study, read Colossians 1:1–8. For more Bible passages on faith, hope, and love, read Romans 5:1–5; 1 Corinthians 13:13; Galatians 5:5–6; 1 Thessalonians 1:3; 5:8; and 1 Peter 1:21–22.

LESSON TWO

PRAYING
WITH POWER

*For this reason, since the day we heard about
you, we have not stopped praying for you.*
COLOSSIANS 1:9

REFLECTION

Right now, all over the world, Christians are praying. In trucks. In elevators. In barracks. Stuck in traffic. Waiting outside ICUs. Talking to God, listening to him, thanking him for amazing blessings, and asking him for "impossible" miracles. Who are the people who faithfully pray for you? Who are the ones you *want* praying for you?

_____

_____

_____

_____

SITUATION

Paul, after providing several reasons as to why he is thankful for the Colossian believers, now states that he has been praying faithfully for them. Paul relates some of the contents of his prayers, which include his requests that God will fill them with wisdom from the Holy Spirit so they may lead lives pleasing to God. He desires for them to grow and mature in Christ—especially so they can persevere in the face of the false teaching in their midst.

OBSERVATION

Read Colossians 1:9–14 from the New International Version or the New King James Version.

NEW INTERNATIONAL VERSION

9 For this reason, since the day we heard about you, we have not stopped praying for you. We continually ask God to fill you with the knowledge of his will through all the wisdom and understanding that the Spirit

gives, [10] so that you may live a life worthy of the Lord and please him in every way: bearing fruit in every good work, growing in the knowledge of God, [11] being strengthened with all power according to his glorious might so that you may have great endurance and patience, [12] and giving joyful thanks to the Father, who has qualified you to share in the inheritance of his holy people in the kingdom of light. [13] For he has rescued us from the dominion of darkness and brought us into the kingdom of the Son he loves, [14] in whom we have redemption, the forgiveness of sins.

New King James Version

[9] For this reason we also, since the day we heard it, do not cease to pray for you, and to ask that you may be filled with the knowledge of His will in all wisdom and spiritual understanding; [10] that you may walk worthy of the Lord, fully pleasing Him, being fruitful in every good work and increasing in the knowledge of God; [11] strengthened with all might, according to His glorious power, for all patience and longsuffering with joy; [12] giving thanks to the Father who has qualified us to be partakers of the inheritance of the saints in the light. [13] He has delivered us from the power of darkness and conveyed us into the kingdom of the Son of His love, [14] in whom we have redemption through His blood, the forgiveness of sins.

EXPLORATION

1. How would you describe your prayer habits for other people?

---

2. What specific requests does Paul make for the Colossian believers?

---

3. Which of these virtues or abilities do you need the most in your life?

_____

_____

_____

_____

4. How do Paul's petitions for the believers in Colossae compare to the kinds of prayers you tend to offer for others?

_____

_____

_____

_____

5. What truths about God and his gifts does Paul mention as the foundation for his requests?

_____

_____

_____

_____

6. Paul's prayers were Christ-focused and God–centered. How does a deep knowledge of God enhance a Christian's prayer life?

_____

_____

_____

_____

INSPIRATION

The key to knowing God's heart is having a relationship with him. A _personal_ relationship. God will speak to you differently than he will speak to others. Just because God spoke to Moses through a burning bush, that doesn't mean we should all sit next to a bush waiting for God to speak. God used a fish to convict Jonah. Does that mean we should have worship services at Sea World? No. God reveals his heart personally to each person.

For that reason, your walk with God is essential. His heart is not seen in an occasional chat or weekly visit. We learn his will as we take up residence in his house every single day.

If you were to take a name at random out of the phone book and ask me, "Max, how does Chester Whomever feel about adultery?" I couldn't answer. I don't know Chester Whomever. But if you were to ask me, "Max, how does Denalyn Lucado feel about adultery?" I wouldn't even have to call her. I know. She's my wife. We have walked together long enough that I know what she thinks.

The same is true with God. Walk with him long enough and you come to know his heart. When you spend time with him in his study, you see his passion. Welcome him to enter the gateway of your soul and you'll perceive his will. (From *The Great House of God* by Max Lucado.)

REACTION

7. Would you characterize your prayer life as a continual conversation with God or an occasional chat? Why?

_____

_____

_____

_____

8. Why do you think believers tend to offer up "safe" prayers (such as praying for a family member's neighbor who is ill) rather than "personal" prayers (such as for their own struggles with pride and envy)? How can you avoid only praying "safe" prayers?

_____

_____

_____

_____

9. What advice would you give a new Christian who is trying to establish a healthy prayer life?

_____

_____

_____

10. What percentage of your prayers is focused on your own needs and desires versus the needs of others?

_____

_____

_____

11. How has having a deep and personal relationship with Christ affected the way you pray?

_____

_____

_____

12. What are two changes you still want to make in your own prayer life?

_____

_____

_____

LIFE LESSONS

Someone once said, "I don't understand much about the great mystery of prayer. I just know this: When I pray, God does amazing things; and when I don't pray, not much happens." Although it's hard to fathom, the Lord has ordained our prayers to play a key role in building of his kingdom! So, what are the basic New Testament guidelines for effective praying? Praying unselfishly and with a pure heart (see James 4:3). Praying relentlessly (see 1 Thessalonians 5:17). Praying and believing that God will work (see Mark 11:24). Praying according to God's will (see John 15:7). And most of all, praying with a heart that is surrendered to God's ultimate purposes (see Luke 22:42).

DEVOTION

God, fill us with the knowledge of your will. Grant us spiritual wisdom and insight so that we might live the kind of lives that please you. Make us fruitful and help us to know you more and more as we live in your infinite strength.

JOURNALING

How would you put Paul's prayer in Colossians 1:9–14 in your own words and personalize it to your life and those in your family?

_____

_____

_____

_____

_____

_____

_____

_____

_____

_____

_____

_____

_____

_____

_____

_____

_____

FOR FURTHER READING

To complete the books of Colossians and Philemon during this twelve-part study, read Colossians 1:9–14. For more Bible passages on prayer, read Psalm 66:18; Mark 1:35; Philippians 4:6– 7; James 1:6; 5:16; and 1 John 3:22.

THE SUPREMACY OF CHRIST

For by [Christ] all things were created that are in heaven and that are on earth, visible and invisible, whether thrones or dominions or principalities or powers. All things were created through Him and for Him.
COLOSSIANS 1:16 NKJV

REFLECTION

History is filled with interesting and remarkable characters. Imagine throwing a dinner party and getting to invite any eight people, living or dead, great or obscure. Who would be on your guest list? Why would you choose to invite those individuals?

SITUATION

Now that Paul has informed the Colossian believers of his prayers from them, he can move into the main subject of his letter: countering the false religious notions and beliefs that have surfaced in the congregation. To do this, he begins by reciting what might have been a hymn in the church (see verses 15–20) that stresses Jesus' supremacy over creation. As God in the flesh, Paul writes, Jesus created and sustains the universe. He is all the Colossian believers will ever need—and he is far superior to any other powers the false teachers have introduced to them.

OBSERVATION

Read Colossians 1:15–23 from the New International Version or the New King James Version.

New International Version

[15] The Son is the image of the invisible God, the firstborn over all creation. [16] For in him all things were created: things in heaven and on earth, visible and invisible, whether thrones or powers or rulers or authorities; all things have been created through him and for him. [17] He is before

all things, and in him all things hold together. [18] And he is the head of the body, the church; he is the beginning and the firstborn from among the dead, so that in everything he might have the supremacy. [19] For God was pleased to have all his fullness dwell in him,[20] and through him to reconcile to himself all things, whether things on earth or things in heaven, by making peace through his blood, shed on the cross.

[21] Once you were alienated from God and were enemies in your minds because of your evil behavior. [22] But now he has reconciled you by Christ's physical body through death to present you holy in his sight, without blemish and free from accusation— [23] if you continue in your faith, established and firm, and do not move from the hope held out in the gospel. This is the gospel that you heard and that has been proclaimed to every creature under heaven, and of which I, Paul, have become a servant.

NEW KING JAMES VERSION

[15] He is the image of the invisible God, the firstborn over all creation. [16] For by Him all things were created that are in heaven and that are on earth, visible and invisible, whether thrones or dominions or principalities or powers. All things were created through Him and for Him. [17] And He is before all things, and in Him all things consist. [18] And He is the head of the body, the church, who is the beginning, the firstborn from the dead, that in all things He may have the preeminence.

[19] For it pleased the Father that in Him all the fullness should dwell, [20] and by Him to reconcile all things to Himself, by Him, whether things on earth or things in heaven, having made peace through the blood of His cross.

[21] And you, who once were alienated and enemies in your mind by wicked works, yet now He has reconciled [22] in the body of His flesh through death, to present you holy, and blameless, and above reproach in His sight— [23] if indeed you continue in the faith, grounded and steadfast, and are not moved away from the hope of the gospel which you heard, which was preached to every creature under heaven, of which I, Paul, became a minister.

EXPLORATION

1. Why do you think Paul chooses to open his letter by quoting this "hymn" to the Colossian believers about the supremacy of Christ?

_____

_____

_____

_____

2. What are some of the key words and phrases that Paul uses to describe Christ's nature?

_____

_____

_____

_____

3. How does this description compare with the way many people in our culture view Christ?

_____

_____

_____

_____

4. What do you think Paul means when he writes that Jesus "is the beginning and the firstborn from among the dead" (verse 18)?

_____

_____

_____

_____

5. In describing Christ's saving work, Paul refers to his readers, before their conversion, as being God's "enemies" (verse 21). Why does he use this term?

_____

_____

_____

6. How do you explain Christ (who he is and what he did) to friends who are not Christians?

_____

_____

_____

INSPIRATION

Make no mistake, Jesus saw himself as God. He leaves us with two options. Accept him as God, or reject him as a megalomaniac. There is no third alternative.

Oh, but we try to create one. Suppose I did the same? Suppose you came across me standing on the side of the road. I can go north or south. You ask me which way I'm going. My reply? "I'm going sorth."

Thinking you didn't hear me correctly, you ask me to repeat the answer.

"I'm going sorth. I can't choose between north and south, so I'm going both. I'm going sorth."

"You can't do that," you reply. "You have to choose."

"Okay," I concede, "I'll head nouth."

"Nouth is not an option!" you insist. "It's either north or south. One way or the other. To the right or to the left. When it comes to this road, you've got to pick."

When it comes to Christ, you've got to do the same. Call him crazy, or crown him as king. Dismiss him as a fraud, or declare him to be God. Walk away from him, or bow down before him. But don't play games with him.

Don't call him a great man. Don't list him among decent folk. Don't clump him with Moses, Elijah, Buddha, Joseph Smith, Muhammad, or Confucius. He didn't leave that option. He is either God or godless. Heaven sent or hell born. All hope or all hype. But nothing in between. (From _Next Door Savior_ by Max Lucado.)

REACTION

7. Do you agree with this idea that you must either accept Jesus as God or reject him as a megalomaniac? Why or why not?

_____

_____

_____

_____

8. How does the fact that "all things have been created through [Christ] and _for him_" (verse 16) affect the way that you lead your life?

_____

_____

_____

_____

9. Paul challenges his readers to continue in the faith and "not move from the hope held out in the gospel" (verse 23). What things have the potential to move you away from Christ today?

_____

_____

_____

_____

10. How can a wrong understanding of Christ's nature or ignorance of his work affect you?

_____

_____

_____

11. What are the most prominent people, things, or desires in your life that compete with Christ's lordship?

12. What are three practical changes can you make in your thinking, schedule, or other area in your life to better to reflect the supremacy of Christ over your life?

LIFE LESSONS

In our noisy and flashy world, it is the "new and improved" that tends to get the attention. We notice big and loud things. We focus on the bizarre and shocking things. And we like upgrades. We are ever looking to trade in and trade up. The more trendy and off-beat something is, the more it appeals to our image-conscious culture. The result is that the "old, old story" of the gospel is increasingly seen as trite and outdated. After all, why follow Jesus—a figure from antiquity—when you can follow the latest New Age guru? The reason, as Paul reminds us, is because Jesus is the beginning and end of everything. All knowledge, power, beauty, mystery, and meaning are found in him. He is the only one who can satisfy the deepest hungers of our hearts. The restless search of the human race ends at the cross of Christ.

DEVOTION

Lord Jesus, thank you for making us and saving us and sustaining us. We enthrone you now as the king of our lives. Give us eyes to see you. Give us ears to hear you. Give us courage to show and share you with the watching world.

JOURNALING

How would you describe what Jesus Christ actually means to you?

_____

_____

_____

_____

_____

_____

_____

_____

_____

_____

_____

_____

_____

_____

_____

_____

_____

_____

_____

FOR FURTHER READING

To complete the books of Colossians and Philemon during this twelve-part study, read Colossians 1:15–23. For more Bible passages on the preeminence of Christ, read John 1:1–18; Ephesians 1:22–23; Hebrews 1:1–3; and Revelation 5:1–14.

LESSON FOUR

SERVING CHRIST

I fill up in my flesh what is still lacking in regard to Christ's afflictions, for the sake of his body, which is the church. I have become its servant by the commission God gave me.
COLOSSIANS 1:24–25

REFLECTION

A principle formed by an Italian economist named Vilfredo Pareto states that in most enterprises, *eighty* percent of the work will be done by *twenty* percent of the people. This same principle can apply to the church—approximately twenty percent of the members do eighty percent of the serving and giving. How do you account for such an imbalance?

SITUATION

In this next portion of Paul's letter, he reflects on his role as a servant of God and his mission to preach the message of Jesus to the Gentile (non-Jewish) churches in the world. In so doing, he reminds the believers in Colossae of the service that others have done to share the true gospel to them. They need to hold on to the truths they have learned like a treasure and not cast them aside when confronted with seemingly more attractive philosophies.

OBSERVATION

Read Colossians 1:24–29 from the New International
Version or the New King James Version.

NEW INTERNATIONAL VERSION

24 Now I rejoice in what I am suffering for you, and I fill up in my flesh what is still lacking in regard to Christ's afflictions, for the sake of his body, which is the church. 25 I have become its servant by the

commission God gave me to present to you the word of God in its fullness— 26 the mystery that has been kept hidden for ages and generations, but is now disclosed to the Lord's people. 27 To them God has chosen to make known among the Gentiles the glorious riches of this mystery, which is Christ in you, the hope of glory.

28 He is the one we proclaim, admonishing and teaching everyone with all wisdom, so that we may present everyone fully mature in Christ. 29 To this end I strenuously contend with all the energy Christ so powerfully works in me.

New King James Version

24 I now rejoice in my sufferings for you, and fill up in my flesh what is lacking in the afflictions of Christ, for the sake of His body, which is the church, 25 of which I became a minister according to the stewardship from God which was given to me for you, to fulfill the word of God, 26 the mystery which has been hidden from ages and from generations, but now has been revealed to His saints. 27 To them God willed to make known what are the riches of the glory of this mystery among the Gentiles: which is Christ in you, the hope of glory. 28 Him we preach, warning every man and teaching every man in all wisdom, that we may present every man perfect in Christ Jesus. 29 To this end I also labor, striving according to His working which works in me mightily.

EXPLORATION

1. How can a person honestly rejoice in the face of sufferings?

2. How does Paul describe the commission given to him by God? How does this motivate all of his actions of service?

3. What is the "mystery" to which Paul refers in verses 26–27?

4. What does it mean to be, as Paul described himself, a servant of the church?

5. How did Paul sum up his mission? In what ways should this be your mission as well?

6. The prophets, apostles, and the early church were devoted to God, all committed to serving him, but were also constantly in trouble. Why do you think Christians face so many trials?

_____

_____

_____

_____

INSPIRATION

The brevity of life grants power to abide, not an excuse to bail. Fleeting days don't justify fleeing problems. Fleeting days strengthen us to endure problems. Will your problems pass? No guarantee they will. Will your pain cease? Perhaps. Perhaps not. But heaven gives this promise: "Our light affliction, which is but for a moment, is working for us a far more exceeding and eternal weight of glory" (2 Corinthians 4:17 NKJV).

The words "weight of glory" conjure up images of the ancient pan scale. Remember the blindfolded lady of justice? She holds a pan scale— two pans, one on either side of the needle. The weight of a purchase would be determined by placing weights on one side and the purchase on the other.

God does the same with your struggles. On one side, he stacks all your burdens. Famines. Firings. Parents who forgot you. Bosses who ignored you. Bad breaks, bad health, bad days. Stack them up and watch one side of the pan scale plummet.

Now witness God's response. Does he remove them? Eliminate the burdens? No. Rather than take them, he offsets them. He places an eternal weight of glory on the other side. Endless joy. Measureless peace. An eternity of him.

Watch what happens as he sets eternity on your scale. Everything changes! The burdens lift. The heavy becomes light when weighed against eternity.

If life is "just for a moment," can't we endure any challenge for a moment?

We can be sick for *just a moment*. We can be lonely for *just a moment*. We can be persecuted for *just a moment*. We can struggle for *just a moment*.

Can't we? Can't we wait for our peace? It's not about us anyway. And it's certainly not about now. (From *It's Not About Me* by Max Lucado.)

REACTION

7. How can focusing on eternity rather than the temporary things of this world put your sufferings in a new and different light?

_____

_____

_____

_____

8. How can a Christian's sufferings actually be beneficial to other believers?

_____

_____

_____

9. What are some of the trials, big and small, that you are currently facing?

_____

_____

_____

10. As you think about tomorrow or the week ahead, what practical difference does it make to know that Christ, "the hope of glory," is in you?

_____

_____

_____

11. As an apostle, Paul served by teaching and preaching. What gifts has God given to you to help you minister and serve others?

_____

_____

_____

_____

12. Christian service involves *laboring* and relying on the Lord's infinite strength. What are some ways you have labored for your church? What fruit did you see from your efforts?

_____

_____

_____

LIFE LESSONS

If Christ were merely *with* us, that would be fantastic. But even more amazing is the declaration that he is *in* us. Think of it—the Prince of Peace, the Good Shepherd, the great I AM—is living in our hearts. The implications are positively staggering! The possibilities are infinite! What did Paul do with such mind-boggling truth? Simple. He served. He poured out his life for others. And why not? After all, the one who filled him (the same one who lives in us) described himself as one who "did not come to be served, but to serve" (see Matthew 20:28). The more we realize the truth of Christ *in us*, the more we are willing to use our gifts and energy to bless others, no matter what hardships come.

DEVOTION

Lord Jesus, thank you for making your home in us. What an amazing mystery, and what a hopeful truth! We can do all things through Christ. Help us to labor in service to others with all the strength that you provide.

JOURNALING

What are some areas in which you need to grow in order to become a better servant for God?

_____

_____

_____

_____

_____

_____

_____

_____

_____

_____

_____

_____

_____

_____

_____

_____

_____

_____

_____

_____

_____

FOR FURTHER READING

To complete the books of Colossians and Philemon during this twelve-part study, read Colossians 1:24–29. For more Bible passages on serving, read Mark 10:43–45; John 13:14; 2 Corinthians 4:11; 12:7–10; Galatians 6:2, 10; Philippians 2:5–8; and 1 Peter 4:10–11.

WALKING WITH CHRIST

*As you therefore have received Christ Jesus
the Lord, so walk in Him, rooted and built
up in Him and established in the faith.*
COLOSSIANS 2:6–7 NKJV

REFLECTION

Perhaps one of the biggest knocks against Christians is the charge that they do not "practice what they preach." It is a curious dilemma. How do you explain the tendency among believers to act one way at certain times and in totally different ways in other settings?

_____

_____

_____

_____

SITUATION

Paul next notes that though he may not have met all of the Colossian believers personally, he has nevertheless labored and contended for each of them so they might know the "mystery of God," which is salvation through Christ. He reminds the believers that only Christ can provide the hidden treasures of wisdom and knowledge they seek—not the other philosophies that may seem attractive to them. In the end, these philosophies are hollow and shallow because they depend on human tradition, rather than the superior wisdom that comes only from God.

OBSERVATION

Read Colossians 2:1–10 from the New International Version or the New King James Version.

New International Version

[1] I want you to know how hard I am contending for you and for those at Laodicea, and for all who have not met me personally. [2] My goal is that they may be encouraged in heart and united in love, so that they may have the full riches of complete understanding, in order that they

may know the mystery of God, namely, Christ, [3] in whom are hidden all the treasures of wisdom and knowledge. [4] I tell you this so that no one may deceive you by fine-sounding arguments. [5] For though I am absent from you in body, I am present with you in spirit and delight to see how disciplined you are and how firm your faith in Christ is.

[6] So then, just as you received Christ Jesus as Lord, continue to live your lives in him, [7] rooted and built up in him, strengthened in the faith as you were taught, and overflowing with thankfulness.

[8] See to it that no one takes you captive through hollow and deceptive philosophy, which depends on human tradition and the elemental spiritual forces of this world rather than on Christ.

[9] For in Christ all the fullness of the Deity lives in bodily form, [10] and in Christ you have been brought to fullness. He is the head over every power and authority.

NEW KING JAMES VERSION

[1] For I want you to know what a great conflict I have for you and those in Laodicea, and for as many as have not seen my face in the flesh, [2] that their hearts may be encouraged, being knit together in love, and attaining to all riches of the full assurance of understanding, to the knowledge of the mystery of God, both of the Father and of Christ, [3] in whom are hidden all the treasures of wisdom and knowledge.

[4] Now this I say lest anyone should deceive you with persuasive words. [5] For though I am absent in the flesh, yet I am with you in spirit, rejoicing to see your good order and the steadfastness of your faith in Christ.

[6] As you therefore have received Christ Jesus the Lord, so walk in Him, [7] rooted and built up in Him and established in the faith, as you have been taught, abounding in it with thanksgiving.

[8] Beware lest anyone cheat you through philosophy and empty deceit, according to the tradition of men, according to the basic principles of the world, and not according to Christ. [9] For in Him dwells all the fullness of the Godhead bodily; [10] and you are complete in Him, who is the head of all principality and power.

EXPLORATION

1. How is it possible to have a deep spiritual concern for people whom you have never met?

_____

_____

_____

_____

2. How can a person learn to distinguish between truth and just fine-sounding arguments?

_____

_____

_____

3. Paul urges his readers toward a more stable faith. What are some practical indications that a person is maturing spiritually?

_____

_____

_____

_____

4. What is Paul's counsel to those who are hungry for true wisdom and spiritual enlightenment?

_____

_____

_____

5. Why is the wisdom that comes from God superior to everything else?

_____

_____

_____

6. Why do you think Paul reiterates throughout this passage that believers are "in Christ"? Why is this idea so significant?

_____

_____

_____

INSPIRATION

Suppose your dad is the world's foremost orthopedic surgeon. People travel from distant countries for him to treat them. Regularly he exchanges damaged joints for healthy ones. With the same confidence that a mechanic changes spark plugs, your dad removes and replaces hips, knees, and shoulders.

At ten years of age you are a bit young to comprehend the accomplishments of a renowned surgeon. But you're not too young to stumble down the stairs and twist your ankle. You roll and writhe on the floor and scream for help. You are weeks away from your first school dance. This is no time for crutches. No time for limping. You need a healthy ankle!

Into the room walks your dad, still wearing his surgical scrubs. He removes your shoe, peels back your sock, and examines the injury. You groan at the sight of the tennis ball–sized bump. Adolescent anxiety kicks in.

"Dad, I'll never walk again!" you say. . . .

Your dad lifts his head and asks you a question. "Do you know what I do for a living?" Actually, you don't. You know he goes to the hospital every day. You know that people call him "doctor." Your mom thinks he is smart. But you don't really know what your father does.

"So," he says as he places a bag of ice on your ankle, "it's time for you to learn." The next day he is waiting for you in the school parking lot. "Hop in. I want you to see what I do," he says. He drives you to his hospital office and shows you the constellation of diplomas on his wall.

Adjacent to them is a collection of awards that include words like distinguished and honorable. He hands you a manual of orthopedic surgery that bears his name. . . .

His cell phone rings. After the call he announces, "We're off to surgery." You scrub up and follow him into the operating room on your crutches. During the next few minutes you have a ringside seat for a procedure in which he reconstructs an ankle. He is the commandant of the operating room. He never hesitates or seeks advice. He just does it.

One of the nurses whispers, "Your dad is the best."

As the two of you ride home that evening, you look at your father. You see him in a different light. If he can conduct orthopedic surgery, he can likely treat a swollen ankle. So you ask, "You think I'll be okay for the dance?"

"Yes, you'll be fine." This time you believe him. . . .

God is king, supreme ruler, absolute monarch, and overlord of all history. An arch of his eyebrow and a million angels will pivot and salute. Every throne is a footstool to his. Every crown is papier-mâché next to his. He consults no advisers. He needs no congress. He reports to no one. He is superior to all others. He is in charge. (From *Anxious for Nothing* by Max Lucado.)

REACTION

7. God is the absolute monarch and overlord of all history. Given this, why do you think so many people seek answers in human philosophies rather than go directly to God?

_____

_____

_____

_____

_____

_____

_____

8. How does picturing God as a world-renown orthopedic surgeon affect you when it comes to believing that he can help you with your problems and concerns?

_____

_____

_____

_____

_____

_____

_____

9. What does it mean to live your life "in Christ" (see Colossians 2:6)? How would you explain how this is done to a brand-new Christian?

_____

_____

_____

_____

_____

_____

10. The Colossians were blessed to have a strong spiritual mentor like Paul. Who are the older and wiser saints in your life who exhort you in the faith?

_____

_____

_____

_____

_____

11. What does it mean to be "brought to fullness" in Christ (verse 10)?

_____

_____

_____

_____

12. Paul uses the metaphor of being "rooted" in Christ (verse 7). How can you develop stronger and deeper spiritual roots this week?

_____

_____

_____

_____

LIFE LESSONS

Like a song stuck on auto play, Paul keeps repeating the same theme over and over again: _Christ is enough because Christ is ultimate._ There is no higher truth. There is no other source of fulfillment. We can search the world over looking for wisdom and spend our lives hunting for meaning and inner peace, but only in Christ do we find the answers that our souls crave. "In [Christ] are hidden all the treasures of wisdom and knowledge" (Colossians 2:3). The search for satisfaction ends at the feet of Jesus. And there, the great journey—the lifelong adventure of faith—begins as we begin our walk with him.

DEVOTION

Lord Jesus, we received you by faith, therefore we must continue to live in you by faith. In a world filled with false ideas, grant us the grace and wisdom to learn to discern. Continually remind us that in you "are all the treasures of wisdom and knowledge."

JOURNALING

What are your biggest struggles in your spiritual walk right now?

FOR FURTHER READING

To complete the books of Colossians and Philemon during this twelve-part study, read Colossians 2:1–10. For more Bible passages on the Christian walk, read John 15:1–11; Romans 6:4; 2 Corinthians 5:7; Galatians 5:16–25; Ephesians 4:1; and 1 John 1:6–7.

LESSON SIX

FOOLISH PHILOSOPHIES

Since you died with Christ to the elemental spiritual
forces of this world, why, as though you still belonged
to the world, do you submit to its rules?
Colossians 2:20

REFLECTION

Survivalist sects and polygamous groups. Hollywood stars trumpeting
Scientology. Atheistic scholars advocating naturalism. Our culture has
almost as many worldviews as we've got people! What anti-Christian
philosophies or extra-biblical religious beliefs are popular in your locale?
Why do you think these philosophies are so attractive to people?

SITUATION

In this section of the letter, Paul continues to remind the Colossian
believers about what they had experienced in Christ. While in their pre-
vious lives they had been ruled by the desires of this world, they had put
those ways to death and experienced the new life that Jesus brings. As a
result of this new life, they had received forgiveness from sin, freedom
from guilt, and authority in Christ. Paul states that those who try to
make them feel "spiritually inferior" by pushing other puffed-up philosophies have themselves lost hold of what is real and true.

OBSERVATION

*Read Colossians 2:11–23 from the New International
Version or the New King James Version.*

New International Version

¹¹ In him you were also circumcised with a circumcision not performed
by human hands. Your whole self ruled by the flesh was put off when

you were circumcised by Christ, [12] having been buried with him in baptism, in which you were also raised with him through your faith in the working of God, who raised him from the dead.

[13] When you were dead in your sins and in the uncircumcision of your flesh, God made you alive with Christ. He forgave us all our sins, [14] having canceled the charge of our legal indebtedness, which stood against us and condemned us; he has taken it away, nailing it to the cross. [15] And having disarmed the powers and authorities, he made a public spectacle of them, triumphing over them by the cross.

[16] Therefore do not let anyone judge you by what you eat or drink, or with regard to a religious festival, a New Moon celebration or a Sabbath day. [17] These are a shadow of the things that were to come; the reality, however, is found in Christ. [18] Do not let anyone who delights in false humility and the worship of angels disqualify you. Such a person also goes into great detail about what they have seen; they are puffed up with idle notions by their unspiritual mind. [19] They have lost connection with the head, from whom the whole body, supported and held together by its ligaments and sinews, grows as God causes it to grow.

[20] Since you died with Christ to the elemental spiritual forces of this world, why, as though you still belonged to the world, do you submit to its rules: [21] "Do not handle! Do not taste! Do not touch!"? [22] These rules, which have to do with things that are all destined to perish with use, are based on merely human commands and teachings. [23] Such regulations indeed have an appearance of wisdom, with their self-imposed worship, their false humility and their harsh treatment of the body, but they lack any value in restraining sensual indulgence.

New King James Version
[11] In Him you were also circumcised with the circumcision made without hands, by putting off the body of the sins of the flesh, by the circumcision of Christ, [12] buried with Him in baptism, in which you also were raised with Him through faith in the working of God, who raised Him from the dead. [13] And you, being dead in your trespasses and the

uncircumcision of your flesh, He has made alive together with Him, having forgiven you all trespasses, [14] having wiped out the handwriting of requirements that was against us, which was contrary to us. And He has taken it out of the way, having nailed it to the cross. [15] Having disarmed principalities and powers, He made a public spectacle of them, triumphing over them in it.

[16] So let no one judge you in food or in drink, or regarding a festival or a new moon or sabbaths, [17] which are a shadow of things to come, but the substance is of Christ. [18] Let no one cheat you of your reward, taking delight in false humility and worship of angels, intruding into those things which he has not seen, vainly puffed up by his fleshly mind, [19] and not holding fast to the Head, from whom all the body, nourished and knit together by joints and ligaments, grows with the increase that is from God.

[20] Therefore, if you died with Christ from the basic principles of the world, why, as though living in the world, do you subject yourselves to regulations— [21] "Do not touch, do not taste, do not handle," [22] which all concern things which perish with the using—according to the commandments and doctrines of men? [23] These things indeed have an appearance of wisdom in self-imposed religion, false humility, and neglect of the body, but are of no value against the indulgence of the flesh.

EXPLORATION

1. How would you explain the difference between the Jewish rite of circumcision and the spiritual circumcision Paul mentions in this passage (see verses 11–12)?

2. What does it mean to be "buried" with Christ and "raised" up in him?

_____

_____

_____

3. Why do you think Paul in his letters always came back to the message of the cross of Christ (see, for example, 1 Corinthians 1:23 and 2:8)?

_____

_____

_____

4. In this passage, Paul talks about some of the religious rules being advocated in ancient Colossae. What legalistic restrictions have you found in your church or spiritual circle?

_____

_____

_____

5. Why do you think religious people and institutions get so uncomfortable with spiritual freedom and try so hard to control others?

_____

_____

_____

6. How can you distinguish between God-honoring spiritual guidelines and human-made religious rules?

_____

_____

_____

INSPIRATION

If you've always thought of Jesus as a pale-faced, milquetoast Tiny Tim, then read Matthew 23 and see the other side: an angry father denouncing the pimps who have prostituted his children. Six times he calls them hypocrites. Five times he calls them blind. Seven times he denounces them and once he prophesies their ruin.

Not what you would call a public relations presentation.

But in the midst of the roaring river of words, there is a safe island of instruction. Somewhere between bursts of fire, Jesus holsters his pistol, turns to the wide-eyed disciples, and describes the essence of simple faith. Four verses: a reading as brief as it is practical. Call it Christ's solution to complicated Christianity.

"But you are not to be called 'Rabbi,' for you have one Teacher, and you are all brothers. And do not call anyone on earth 'father,' for you have one Father, and he is in heaven. Nor are you to be called instructors, for you have one Instructor, the Messiah. The greatest among you will be your servant. For those who exalt themselves will be humbled, and those who humble themselves will be exalted" (Matthew 23:8–12).

How do you simplify your faith? How do you get rid of the clutter? How do you discover a joy worth waking up to? Simple. Get rid of the middleman.

Discover truth for yourself. "You have one Teacher, and you are all brothers" (verse 8).

Develop trust for yourself. "Do not call anyone on earth 'father,' for you have one Father, and he is in heaven" (verse 9).

Discern his will for yourself. "You have one Instructor, the Messiah" (verse 10).

There are some who position themselves between you and God. There are some who suggest the only way to get to God is through them. There is the great teacher who has the final word on Bible teaching. There is the father who must bless your acts. There is the spiritual master who will tell you what God wants you to do.

Jesus' message for complicated religion is to remove these middle-men. He's not saying that you don't need teachers, elders, or counselors. He is saying, however, that we are all brothers and sisters and have equal access to the Father. Simplify your faith by seeking God for yourself. No confusing ceremonies necessary. No mysterious rituals required. No elaborate channels of command or levels of access.

You have a Bible? You can study. You have a heart? You can pray. You have a mind? You can think. (From *And the Angels Were Silent* by Max Lucado.)

REACTION

7. When it comes to matters of faith, how much do you rely on God's indwelling Spirit to be your Counselor and Guide? How much do you just do what other Christians tell you to do?

8. How can you and your church steer clear of the dangerous ways of legalism?

9. How can you avoid being swept away by the subtle winds of spiritual error?

10. The Colossian believers were influenced by *asceticism*—the shunning of anything that might result in physical pleasure or comfort. What is so seemingly "spiritual" about such a lifestyle?

_____

_____

_____

11. The worship of angels was an ancient practice. Why do angels appeal to people today? What do you think was attractive to people during Paul's day in praying to angels?

_____

_____

_____

12. Why are external rules incapable of bringing about internal reformation in a person?

_____

_____

LIFE LESSONS

As followers of Jesus, we must remain on high alert. Both the Bible and history show how easy it is for well-meaning but naïve Christians to become sidetracked by the exotic claims of religious cults and the pride-enticing allure of modern philosophies. Only one person is worthy of our minds' attention and our hearts' affection: Jesus Christ. "What is true and real has come and is found in" him (Colossians 2:17 NCV). If you are laboring in vain to keep a long list of human-made religious rules, if you are confused by the competing claims of fast-talking spiritual gurus, remember that Christ came to set us free. Push aside the spiritual static of all the other voices. Open the Gospels and listen again to the still, small voice of Christ.

DEVOTION

Father in heaven, thank you for revealing yourself in Christ. Not only did he die for our sins, but he also rose again to show us how we need to live and where we need to go. Help us to grow in our faith so we can distinguish between the genuine leading of your Spirit and the counterfeit promptings of the evil one.

JOURNALING

Do you engage in any activities on which other Christians frown? How do you know if they are being legalistic toward you or if you are being too lax in your faith?

FOR FURTHER READING

To complete the books of Colossians and Philemon during this twelve-part study, read Colossians 2:11–23. For more Bible passages on suspect spirituality, read 1 Timothy 4:1–7; 2 Timothy 3:1–9; Titus 1:10–16; 2 Peter 2:1–22; 2 John 7–11; and Jude 1:3–16.

LIVING DIFFERENTLY

*If then you were raised with Christ, seek those
things which are above, where Christ is, sitting
at the right hand of God. Set your mind on
things above, not on things on the earth.*
COLOSSIANS 3:1–2 NKJV

REFLECTION

Inner fulfillment. A new and different life. This is what we all want to find. What else can explain the way some people change churches, move on from relationships, and swap jobs? What else could account for the way people consume goods, the boom in plastic surgery, or the growth of certain cults? What are the biggest and most satisfying changes you've undergone?

_____

_____

_____

_____

SITUATION

Paul continues in this section of his letter to remind the believers in Colossae of the benefits of the new life they have received in Christ—and how walking in this new life should reflect a change in their attitudes and behaviors. They had died to their former ways when they accepted Christ, so they needed to not only put all other foolish philosophies aside, but they also needed to live in a way that reflected they belonged to God and had Christ within them. After all, if indeed they had been transformed, their lifestyle should reflect the change.

OBSERVATION

Read Colossians 3:1–17 from the New International Version or the New King James Version.

NEW INTERNATIONAL VERSION
¹ Since, then, you have been raised with Christ, set your hearts on things above, where Christ is, seated at the right hand of God. ² Set your

minds on things above, not on earthly things. [3] For you died, and your life is now hidden with Christ in God. [4] When Christ, who is your life, appears, then you also will appear with him in glory.

[5] Put to death, therefore, whatever belongs to your earthly nature: sexual immorality, impurity, lust, evil desires and greed, which is idolatry. [6] Because of these, the wrath of God is coming. [7] You used to walk in these ways, in the life you once lived. [8] But now you must also rid yourselves of all such things as these: anger, rage, malice, slander, and filthy language from your lips. [9] Do not lie to each other, since you have taken off your old self with its practices [10] and have put on the new self, which is being renewed in knowledge in the image of its Creator. [11] Here there is no Gentile or Jew, circumcised or uncircumcised, barbarian, Scythian, slave or free, but Christ is all, and is in all.

[12] Therefore, as God's chosen people, holy and dearly loved, clothe yourselves with compassion, kindness, humility, gentleness and patience. [13] Bear with each other and forgive one another if any of you has a grievance against someone. Forgive as the Lord forgave you. [14] And over all these virtues put on love, which binds them all together in perfect unity.

[15] Let the peace of Christ rule in your hearts, since as members of one body you were called to peace. And be thankful. [16] Let the message of Christ dwell among you richly as you teach and admonish one another with all wisdom through psalms, hymns, and songs from the Spirit, singing to God with gratitude in your hearts. [17] And whatever you do, whether in word or deed, do it all in the name of the Lord Jesus, giving thanks to God the Father through him.

New King James Version

[1] If then you were raised with Christ, seek those things which are above, where Christ is, sitting at the right hand of God. [2] Set your mind on things above, not on things on the earth. [3] For you died, and your life is hidden with Christ in God. [4] When Christ who is our life appears, then you also will appear with Him in glory.

⁵ Therefore put to death your members which are on the earth: fornication, uncleanness, passion, evil desire, and covetousness, which is idolatry. ⁶ Because of these things the wrath of God is coming upon the sons of disobedience, ⁷ in which you yourselves once walked when you lived in them.

⁸ But now you yourselves are to put off all these: anger, wrath, malice, blasphemy, filthy language out of your mouth. ⁹ Do not lie to one another, since you have put off the old man with his deeds, ¹⁰ and have put on the new man who is renewed in knowledge according to the image of Him who created him, ¹¹ where there is neither Greek nor Jew, circumcised nor uncircumcised, barbarian, Scythian, slave nor free, but Christ is all and in all.

¹² Therefore, as the elect of God, holy and beloved, put on tender mercies, kindness, humility, meekness, longsuffering; ¹³ bearing with one another, and forgiving one another, if anyone has a complaint against another; even as Christ forgave you, so you also must do. ¹⁴ But above all these things put on love, which is the bond of perfection. ¹⁵ And let the peace of God rule in your hearts, to which also you were called in one body; and be thankful. ¹⁶ Let the word of Christ dwell in you richly in all wisdom, teaching and admonishing one another in psalms and hymns and spiritual songs, singing with grace in your hearts to the Lord. ¹⁷ And whatever you do in word or deed, do all in the name of the Lord Jesus, giving thanks to God the Father through Him.

EXPLORATION

1. How does a person seek or set his or her mind on those things that are from above?

2. What does Paul mean when he says that your life "is hidden with Christ in God" (verse 3 NKJV) and that "Christ . . . is your life" (verse 4)?

_____

_____

_____

_____

_____

_____

3. What are some of the ways of life that the believers needed to put to death? What was the problem with them holding on to these former ways?

_____

_____

_____

_____

_____

4. Paul contrasts two ways of life—an old way and a new way, with Christ making the difference. In what ways has Christ made such a radical difference in your life?

_____

_____

_____

_____

_____

5. What aspects of the new life in Christ do you need to "wear" more consistently?

_____

_____

_____

_____

6. It almost sounds in this passage as if Paul is saying, "You want to change? Okay, then stop sinning." Why is this so easy to say but often so difficult to do?

_____

_____

_____

INSPIRATION

Accept this invitation of Jesus: "Abide in My love" (John 15:9 NASB). When you abide somewhere, you live there. You grow familiar with the surroundings. You don't pull in the driveway and ask, "Where is the garage?" You don't consult the blueprint to find the kitchen. To abide is to be at home.

To abide in Christ's love is to make his love your home. Not a roadside park or hotel room you occasionally visit, but your preferred dwelling. You rest in him. Eat in him. When thunder claps, you step beneath his roof. His walls secure you from the winds. His fireplace warms you from the winters of life. As John urged, "We take up permanent residence in a life of love" (1 John 4:16 MSG). You abandon the old house of false love and move into his home of real love.

Adapting to this new home takes time. First few nights in a new home you can wake up and walk into a wall. I did. Not in a new home, but in a motel. Climbed out of bed to get a glass of water, turned left, and flattened my nose. The dimensions to the room were different.

The dimensions of God's love are different too. You've lived a life in a house of imperfect love. You think God is going to cut you as the coach did, or abandon you as your father did, or judge you as false religion did, or curse you as your friend did. He won't, but it takes time to be convinced.

For that reason, abide in him. Hang on to Christ the same way a branch clutches the vine. According to Jesus, the branch models his definition of *abiding*. "As the branch cannot bear fruit of itself unless it abides in the vine, so neither can you unless you abide in Me" (John 15:4 NASB). (From *Come Thirsty* by Max Lucado.)

REACTION

7. Do you feel "at home in Christ"? Why or why not?

_____

_____

_____

_____

8. Of the wrong attitudes and actions that Paul mentions, which habits do you most struggle with the most? Why do you think this is the case?

_____

_____

_____

_____

9. Paul wrote the words of Colossians 3:12–17 to "God's chosen people," which represents the whole church. Does his description fit your church or small group? Why or why not?

_____

_____

_____

_____

10. How well do you tend to bear with others and forgive them? Why is it critical to forgive others in the body of Christ as the Lord has forgiven you?

_____

_____

_____

_____

11. What relationship in your life is currently giving you the most trouble? Why do you think this is the case?

_____

_____

_____

12. How can you cultivate a more thankful attitude in life? What practical steps would you need to take to make that happen?

_____

_____

_____

LIFE LESSONS

Call it what you will—the gospel message or the Christian faith—but the fact is the kind of spirituality advocated by Christ was never meant to be a neat religious theory. As someone has said, Jesus didn't come to give us a lot of new *information*; rather, he came that we might undergo *transformation*. He does this by first forgiving us and wiping the slate clean. Then he does something odd but powerful. He moves us into himself and moves himself into us. In other words, we are united with him fundamentally and eternally. He becomes both our life and our Lord. And he will never rest until we are changed and our character is just like his.

DEVOTION

Father, what a wonderful promise you have given that the good work you begun in us will continue until completion. Thank you for new life. We open our hearts to you and invite you to do your transforming work within us. We want to make our home in you, and we want you to be at home in us.

JOURNALING

As you look at Paul's words in Colossians 3:12–17, how would you respond about your obedience to each of these commands that he sets forth?

FOR FURTHER READING

To complete the books of Colossians and Philemon during this twelve-part study, read Colossians 3:1–17. For more Bible passages on holy living, read Psalm 15:1–5; Ephesians 5:1–19; Philippians 4:1–9; 1 Thessalonians 4:1–12; and 1 Peter 4:1–11.

HOME, SWEET HOME

*Wives, submit yourselves to your husbands,
as is fitting in the Lord. Husbands, love your
wives and do not be harsh with them.*
COLOSSIANS 3:18–19

REFLECTION

A number of surveys indicate the divorce rate among Christians is not substantially lower than that of the general population. Other studies suggest that many of the problems that plague irreligious families are also common in Christian families. How do you account for these facts? Why do think the gospel seems to be so irrelevant in many Christian homes?

_____

_____

_____

SITUATION

The apostle Paul, having concluded his general instructions to his readers on how to live as God's chosen people, now moves to address some specific issues on how Christians are to conduct themselves in the home. These instructions, commonly known as the "household code," appear in similar forms in Paul's other letters (see Ephesians 5:21–6:9, 1 Timothy 2:8–15, Titus 2:1–10) and also in the general epistles (see 1 Peter 2:11–3:12). However, the instructions in Colossians is unique in that it points directly to Christ—believers are to conduct themselves in such a manner because it is ultimately Jesus whom they are striving to serve.

OBSERVATION

Read Colossians 3:18–21 from the New International Version or the New King James Version.

NEW INTERNATIONAL VERSION
[18] Wives, submit yourselves to your husbands, as is fitting in the Lord.
[19] Husbands, love your wives and do not be harsh with them.

²⁰ Children, obey your parents in everything, for this pleases the Lord.

²¹ Fathers, do not embitter your children, or they will become discouraged.

NEW KING JAMES VERSION

¹⁸ Wives, submit to your own husbands, as is fitting in the Lord.

¹⁹ Husbands, love your wives and do not be bitter toward them.

²⁰ Children, obey your parents in all things, for this is well pleasing to the Lord.

²¹ Fathers, do not provoke your children, lest they become discouraged.

EXPLORATION

1. Why do you think there is controversy regarding the biblical command for wives to submit to the authority of their husbands?

2. How might most of this furor subside if men humbly and consistently lived out Paul's commanded to love their wives and not be bitter toward them?

3. What connection does Paul make between children obeying their parents and pleasing God?

4. What were the rules your parents made you obey as a child? Looking back, can you see how these rules were made for your own good? Why or why not?

_____

_____

_____

_____

5. What are some ways that parents nag their children or provoke them to discouragement?

_____

_____

_____

_____

6. What marriages or families do you most admire? Why?

_____

_____

_____

INSPIRATION

Every time we ate at home, my mom gave my brother and me the same instructions: "Put a little bit of everything on your plate."

We never had to be told to clean the plate. Eating volume was not a challenge. Variety was. Don't get me wrong, Mom was a good cook. But boiled okra? Asparagus? More like "croak-ra" and "gasp-aragus." Were they really intended for human consumption?

According to Mom, they were, and—according to Mom—they had to be eaten. "Eat some of everything." That was the rule in our house.

But that was not the rule at the cafeteria. On special occasions, we made the forty-five-minute drive to the greatest culinary innovation since the gas stove: the cafeteria line. Ah, what a fine moment indeed to take a tray and gaze down the midway at the endless options. A veritable cornucopia of fine cuisine.

Down the row you walk, intoxicated by the selection and liberated by the freedom. Yes to the fried fish; no to the fried tomatoes. Yes to the pecan pie; no, no, a thousand times no to the "croak-ra" and "gasp-aragus." Cafeteria lines are great.

Wouldn't it be nice if love were like a cafeteria line? What if you could look at a person with whom you live and select what you want and pass on what you don't? What if parents could do this with kids? "I'll take a plate of good grades and cute smiles, and I'm passing on the teenage identity crisis and tuition bills."

What if kids could do the same with parents? "Please give me a helping of allowances and free lodging but no rules or curfews, thank you."

And spouse with spouse? "Hmm, how about a bowl of good health and good moods. But job transfers, in-laws, and laundry are not on my diet."

Wouldn't it be great if love were like a cafeteria line? It would be easier. It would be neater. It would be painless and peaceful. But you know what? It wouldn't be love. Love doesn't accept just a few things. Love is willing to accept all things.

God's view of love is like my mom's view of food. When we love someone, we take the entire package. No picking and choosing. No large helpings of the good and passing on the bad. Love is a package deal. (From *A Love Worth Giving* by Max Lucado.)

REACTION

7. How well is your family showing love to each other right now?

_____

_____

_____

_____

8. Why does submitting or deferring to someone else in your life *not* imply that you are inferior to that person (see 1 Corinthians 11:3)?

_____

_____

_____

_____

9. In Ephesians 5:25, Paul writes, "Husbands, love your wives, just as Christ loved the church and gave himself up for her." How does this expand and elaborate on his command to the Colossian believers that husbands are to love their wives?

_____

_____

_____

_____

10. How do you define parental discipline? How have you seen this used effectively and ineffectively in your life?

_____

_____

_____

11. What are some of the most discouraging things you see parents do to their kids?

_____

_____

_____

12. What three actions could you take today that would immediately make your home more peaceful, loving, and God honoring?

_____

_____

_____

LIFE LESSONS

Someone once said, "If our faith doesn't work at home, our faith doesn't work." Nowhere is it more crucial that we put our beliefs into practice and on display than in the home. So today, ask yourself a few hard questions. Is your relationship with Jesus noticeable by the way you talk to your family members? By the way in which you listen? How about in the way you resolve conflicts? Is your family happy to see you come home, or secretly more glad to see you leave? Do you serve your spouse and encourage your kids? Is there an atmosphere of respect and gentleness in your home? When was the last time you made a sacrifice for someone else by putting his or her needs before your own desires?

DEVOTION

Father, we could use some home improvements in our family. Remind us that we can't change anyone but ourselves, and that we can't even do that without your help. Strengthen us today to do our part—to fulfill our family role in a way that pleases you and promotes peace.

JOURNALING

What are your best memories from your growing-up years with your family?

FOR FURTHER READING

To complete the books of Colossians and Philemon during this twelve-part study, read Colossians 3:18–21. For more Bible passages on the home and family, read Genesis 2:23–24; Deuteronomy 5:16; Psalm 127:3; Ephesians 5:22–6:4; 1 Timothy 3:4, 11, 15; and 1 Peter 3:1–7.

WHAT ABOUT WORK?

*Whatever you do, do it heartily, as to the Lord
and not to men, knowing that from the Lord you
will receive the reward of the inheritance.*
COLOSSIANS 3:23–24 NKJV

REFLECTION

Many people in our society view their jobs as just a necessary evil. They don't enjoy what they are doing, but at least it pays the bills! What about you? How would you summarize your feelings about your current occupation or vocation?

SITUATION

In Paul's day, approximately fifty percent of the residents of the Roman Empire were slaves. Although Paul does not directly oppose this practice in his letters, he does remind his readers that *everyone* has value in the family of Christ—regardless of their economic or social position—and that people are to treat each other with respect. In this passage in Colossians, we find how Christ makes a difference in master-slave relationships, and also some great principles for how Christian employers and employees should live and interact.

OBSERVATION

Read Colossians 3:22–4:1 from the New International Version or the New King James Version.

New International Version

²² Slaves, obey your earthly masters in everything; and do it, not only when their eye is on you and to curry their favor, but with sincerity of heart and reverence for the Lord. ²³ Whatever you do, work at it with all

your heart, as working for the Lord, not for human masters, [24] since you know that you will receive an inheritance from the Lord as a reward. It is the Lord Christ you are serving. [25] Anyone who does wrong will be repaid for their wrongs, and there is no favoritism.

[4:1] Masters, provide your slaves with what is right and fair, because you know that you also have a Master in heaven.

NEW KING JAMES VERSION

[22] Bondservants, obey in all things your masters according to the flesh, not with eye service, as men-pleasers, but in sincerity of heart, fearing God. [23] And whatever you do, do it heartily, as to the Lord and not to men, [24] knowing that from the Lord you will receive the reward of the inheritance; for you serve the Lord Christ. [25] But he who does wrong will be repaid for what he has done, and there is no partiality.

[4:1] Masters, give your bondservants what is just and fair, knowing that you also have a Master in heaven.

EXPLORATION

1. Why do you think Paul and the other apostles didn't completely condemn slavery?

_____

_____

_____

_____

2. What appeal does Paul make to slaves to obey their masters?

_____

_____

_____

_____

3. What instructions does Paul give to masters on how to treat their slaves?

_____

_____

_____

4. What reasons does Paul give for striving for excellence in your work?

_____

_____

_____

5. In what ways are you pursuing excellence in your work? How does it help to know that ultimately you are working for the Lord and not any human bosses?

_____

_____

_____

6. What is the best job you've ever had? Who is the best boss or employer you've ever had? What impressed you the most about that job and that employer?

_____

_____

_____

INSPIRATION

Heaven's calendar has seven Sundays a week. God sanctifies each day. He conducts holy business at all hours and in all places. He uncommons the common by turning kitchen sinks into shrines, cafés into convents, and nine-to-five workdays into spiritual adventures.

Workdays? Yes, workdays. He ordained your work as something good. Before he gave Adam a wife or a child, even before he gave Adam britches, God gave Adam a job. "Then the LORD God took the man and put him into the garden of Eden to cultivate it and keep it" (Genesis 2:15 NASB). Innocence, not indolence, characterized the first family.

God views work worthy of its own engraved commandment: "You shall work six days, but on the seventh day you shall rest" (Exodus 34:21 NASB). We like the second half of that verse. But emphasis on the day of rest might cause us to miss the command of work: "You shall work six days." Whether you work at home or in the marketplace, your work matters to God.

And your work matters to society. We need you! Cities need plumbers. Nations need soldiers. Stoplights break. Bones break. We need people to repair the first and set the second. Someone has to raise kids, raise cane, and manage the kids who raise Cain.

Whether you log on or lace up for the day, you imitate God. The Lord himself worked for the first six days of creation. Jesus said, "My Father is always at his work to this very day, and I too am working" (John 5:17). Your career consumes half of your lifetime. Shouldn't it broadcast God? Don't those forty to sixty hours a week belong to him as well? (From *Cure for the Common Life* by Max Lucado.)

REACTION

7. Do you have a hard time viewing work as a spiritual activity? Why or why not?

_____

_____

_____

8. What is the proper motivation for work?

_____

_____

_____

9. What factors make you unmotivated at work and tempt you to do less than your best?

_____

_____

_____

10. If you were an employer, what practices or policies would you implement to stimulate your workers to do their best?

_____

_____

_____

11. Who is the hardest-working person you know? What makes him or her such a good worker?

_____

_____

_____

12. What are three practical things you can do today to help develop a better attitude regarding your job, your supervisor, or your coworkers?

_____

_____

_____

LIFE LESSONS

Unless you were born with a silver spoon in your mouth and a pile of gold bullion in the bank, you will have to work—and perhaps even _labor_ and _toil_ in this life. This isn't a pleasant thought, but it's true nonetheless. Every occupation in a fallen world—working alongside fallen coworkers and for fallen bosses—involves frustration and calls for tough choices. We can work grimly or gladly, make mediocrity our goal, or we can commit ourselves to excellence. Paul tells us that Christians should never do just enough to get by. We should do our work "heartily" (Colossians 3:23 NKJV)—with a good attitude and all-out effort. After all, it is the Lord Christ whom we serve, and to whom we will one day give an account (see 2 Corinthians 5:10).

DEVOTION

Lord, thank you for the reminder that our occupations matter to you. This week, in our attitude, in our work ethic, and in our habits, may we make you smile. And, as a bonus, may we have a positive impact on those in our workplaces. Those are wages enough.

JOURNALING

How can a person know when it is time to seek different employment?

FOR FURTHER READING

To complete the books of Colossians and Philemon during this twelve-part study, read Colossians 3:22–4:1. For more Bible passages on work, see Genesis 3:19; Deuteronomy 24:15; Proverbs 10:4; 12:11; 22:29; Ephesians 6:5–9; 1 Timothy 6:1; Titus 2:9; and 1 Peter 2:18.

A MOUTH THAT MAKES A DIFFERENCE

Let your conversation be always full of grace, seasoned with salt, so that you may know how to answer everyone.
COLOSSIANS 4:6

REFLECTION

Today, we call sharing the gospel with other people by many names: *evangelism, witnessing, soul-winning, giving a testimony.* What images—positive or negative—come to mind when you hear someone refer to "sharing the gospel"?

_____

_____

_____

_____

SITUATION

Paul wraps up the main body of his letter by encouraging the Colossian believers to devote themselves to prayer and to be "watchful" for the work God is doing in the world. He also requests for them to pray that he will continue to be able to share the message of Christ to a hurting and lost world—which was a definite concern of his at the time, since he wrote this letter from a prison cell. Paul's challenge to the believers—and to us—is for them to open their mouths and boldly (yet gently) speak the only truth that sets people free.

OBSERVATION

Read Colossians 4:2–6 from the New International Version or the New King James Version.

NEW INTERNATIONAL VERSION

² Devote yourselves to prayer, being watchful and thankful. ³ And pray for us, too, that God may open a door for our message, so that we may proclaim the mystery of Christ, for which I am in chains. ⁴ Pray that I

may proclaim it clearly, as I should. [5] Be wise in the way you act toward outsiders; make the most of every opportunity. [6] Let your conversation be always full of grace, seasoned with salt, so that you may know how to answer everyone.

NEW KING JAMES VERSION

[2] Continue earnestly in prayer, being vigilant in it with thanksgiving; [3] meanwhile praying also for us, that God would open to us a door for the word, to speak the mystery of Christ, for which I am also in chains, [4] that I may make it manifest, as I ought to speak.

[5] Walk in wisdom toward those who are outside, redeeming the time. [6] Let your speech always be with grace, seasoned with salt, that you may know how you ought to answer each one.

EXPLORATION

1. What does it mean to "devote" yourself to prayer? What does this look like in your life?

_____

_____

_____

2. Some have suggested it is important for believers to talk to God about people before they talk to people about God. Why do you think this is true?

_____

_____

3. How can you tell when God has presented an opportunity for you to share the gospel?

_____

_____

_____

4. What exactly is the "clear and simple" gospel that Paul wanted to proclaim?

_____

_____

_____

_____

5. How proactively do you look for opportunities to turn conversations toward spiritual issues? What tends to get in the way of seeing these opportunities?

_____

_____

_____

_____

6. What do you think Paul means when he says that a Christian's conversation with an unbeliever should be "seasoned with salt" (verse 6)?

_____

_____

_____

INSPIRATION

Think about your first encounter with the Christ. Robe yourself in that moment. Resurrect the relief. Recall the purity. Summon forth the passion. Can you remember?

I can. 1965. A red-headed ten-year-old with a tornado of freckles sits in a Bible class on a Wednesday night. What I remember of the class are scenes—school desks with initials carved in them. A blackboard. A dozen or so kids, some listening, some not. A teacher wearing a suit coat too tight to button around his robust belly.

He is talking about Jesus. He is explaining the cross. I know I had heard it before, but that night I heard it for sure. "You can't save yourself; you need a savior." I can't explain why it connected that night as opposed to another, but it did. The teacher simply articulated what I was beginning to understand—I was lost—and he explained what I needed—a redeemer. From that night on, my heart belonged to Jesus.

Many would argue that a ten-year-old is too young for such a decision. And they may be right. All I know is that I never made a more earnest decision in my life. I didn't know much about God, but what I knew was enough. I knew I wanted to go to heaven. And I knew I couldn't do it alone.

No one had to tell me to be happy. No one had to tell me to tell others. They couldn't keep me quiet. I told all my friends at school. I put a bumper sticker on my bicycle. And though I'd never read 2 Corinthians 4:13, I knew what it meant. "I believed; therefore I have spoken." Pardon truly received is pardon powerfully proclaimed.

There is a direct correlation between the accuracy of our memory and the effectiveness of our mission. If we are not teaching people how to be saved, it is perhaps because we have forgotten the tragedy of being lost! If we're not teaching the message of forgiveness, it may be because we don't remember what it was like to be guilty. And if we're not preaching the cross, it could be that we've subconsciously decided that—God forbid—somehow we don't need it. (From *Six Hours One Friday* by Max Lucado.)

REACTION

7. What have been your experiences with trying to communicate your faith in Christ? What is your current practice?

_____

_____

_____

_____

_____

8. How consistently do you pray that God would open doors for the gospel message to be shared?

9. What are some signs that God is working in a person's heart and bringing him or her to himself?

10. What exactly needs to be "clear" about the way you present the gospel?

11. What are some wise and unwise ways you can act around those who do not yet share your faith?

12. How equipped or prepared do you feel when it comes to articulating what you believe?

LIFE LESSONS

It's important to remember that we can use our tongues for ill or for good. We can gossip and criticize and withhold truth, or we can impact others positively by speaking to them about the life-changing love of Christ. If we want to use our mouths to make an eternal difference (and deep down, every Christian does), we must begin with preparation and prayer. Make sure, first, that you know how to give a reason for the spiritual hope that is in you (see 1 Peter 3:15). Consider attending an evangelism training workshop or working with a fellow Christian with many years of experience of sharing his or her faith. Second, make it your daily practice to pray for opportunities to clearly tell others the good news of forgiveness and new life in Christ.

DEVOTION

Father, life is so short. Remind us daily that we have been given a great treasure and an urgent task—to tell others about your grace and love. Make us wise in the way we act around unbelievers. May we be courageous, kind, and clear in our conversations.

JOURNALING

Think about the people in your life who do not know Christ but show signs of being interested in the gospel. What approach could you take with each person in talking about spiritual things?

_____

_____

_____

_____

_____

_____

_____

FOR FURTHER READING

To complete the books of Colossians and Philemon during this twelve-part study, read Colossians 4:2–6. For more Bible passages on making the most of witnessing opportunities, read Mark 5:18–19; John 9:4; Acts 21:37–22:1; 1 Corinthians 2:1–5; and Ephesians 5:15–16.

COMPANIONS ON THE JOURNEY

These are my only fellow workers for the kingdom of God who are of the circumcision; they have proved to be a comfort to me.
COLOSSIANS 4:11 NKJV

REFLECTION

The Bible uses a variety of metaphors to describe the church: a body (1 Corinthians 12), a living building (Ephesians 2:19–22), a temple (2 Cor. 6:16), a spiritual family (John 1:12; 1 John 3:1), a bride (2 Cor. 11:2), and a flock (Acts 20:29). If you were to come up with a symbol or metaphor to describe your local church, what would it be?

_____

_____

_____

SITUATION

Paul concludes his letter to the Colossian church with some final greetings from a variety of colleagues and mutual friends, including Epaphras, who likely founded the Colossian church and served as Paul's link to what was happening in their community. In these closing words from Paul, we are each reminded that the Christian faith should bring believers *together* as a single body. God means for his children to live and grow and serve in unity.

OBSERVATION

Read Colossians 4:7–18 from the New International Version or the New King James Version.

NEW INTERNATIONAL VERSION

[7] Tychicus will tell you all the news about me. He is a dear brother, a faithful minister and fellow servant in the Lord. [8] I am sending him to you for the express purpose that you may know about our circumstances

and that he may encourage your hearts. [9] He is coming with Onesimus, our faithful and dear brother, who is one of you. They will tell you everything that is happening here.

[10] My fellow prisoner Aristarchus sends you his greetings, as does Mark, the cousin of Barnabas. (You have received instructions about him; if he comes to you, welcome him.) [11] Jesus, who is called Justus, also sends greetings. These are the only Jews among my co-workers for the kingdom of God, and they have proved a comfort to me. [12] Epaphras, who is one of you and a servant of Christ Jesus, sends greetings. He is always wrestling in prayer for you, that you may stand firm in all the will of God, mature and fully assured. [13] I vouch for him that he is working hard for you and for those at Laodicea and Hierapolis. [14] Our dear friend Luke, the doctor, and Demas send greetings. [15] Give my greetings to the brothers and sisters at Laodicea, and to Nympha and the church in her house.

[16] After this letter has been read to you, see that it is also read in the church of the Laodiceans and that you in turn read the letter from Laodicea.

[17] Tell Archippus: "See to it that you complete the ministry you have received in the Lord."

[18] I, Paul, write this greeting in my own hand. Remember my chains. Grace be with you.

New King James Version

[7] Tychicus, a beloved brother, faithful minister, and fellow servant in the Lord, will tell you all the news about me. [8] I am sending him to you for this very purpose, that he may know your circumstances and comfort your hearts, [9] with Onesimus, a faithful and beloved brother, who is one of you. They will make known to you all things which are happening here.

[10] Aristarchus my fellow prisoner greets you, with Mark the cousin of Barnabas (about whom you received instructions: if he comes to you, welcome him), [11] and Jesus who is called Justus. These are my only fellow workers for the kingdom of God who are of the circumcision; they have proved to be a comfort to me.

¹² Epaphras, who is one of you, a bondservant of Christ, greets you, always laboring fervently for you in prayers, that you may stand perfect and complete in all the will of God. ¹³ For I bear him witness that he has a great zeal for you, and those who are in Laodicea, and those in Hierapolis. ¹⁴ Luke the beloved physician and Demas greet you. ¹⁵ Greet the brethren who are in Laodicea, and Nymphas and the church that is in his house.

¹⁶ Now when this epistle is read among you, see that it is read also in the church of the Laodiceans, and that you likewise read the epistle from Laodicea. ¹⁷ And say to Archippus, "Take heed to the ministry which you have received in the Lord, that you may fulfill it."

¹⁸ This salutation by my own hand—Paul. Remember my chains. Grace be with you. Amen.

EXPLORATION

1. Who are your dearest brothers and sisters in the faith? What makes them important in your life?

_____

_____

2. How do you think other Christians would describe you in a letter to a third party?

_____

_____

3. Why are warm greetings and words of affirmation so important among believers?

_____

_____

4. Why did Paul feel the need to mention that Aristarchus, Mark, and Jesus (who was called Justus) were Jewish believers?

_____

_____

_____

5. What special words did Paul have for Archippus? Why do you think he felt it was necessary to include this instruction?

_____

_____

_____

6. What is the last letter, email, or text that you wrote in which your goal was solely to offer spiritual encouragement?

_____

_____

_____

INSPIRATION

The Bible has its share of saints, spurred by a gut-level conviction that they had been called by no one less than God himself. As a result, their work wasn't affected by moods, cloudy days, or rocky trails. Their performance graph didn't rise and fall with roller-coaster irregularity. They weren't addicted to accolades or applause nor deterred by grumpy bosses or empty wallets. Rather than strive to be spectacular, they aspired to be accountable and dependable. And since their loyalty was not determined by their comfort, they were just as faithful in dark prisons as they were in spotlighted pulpits.

Reliable servants. They're the binding of the Bible. Their acts are rarely recited and their names are seldom mentioned. Yet were it not for their loyal devotion to God, many great events never would have occurred . . .

Epaphras would be on this list. . . . To describe this fellow with the longer five-syllable name (Epaphroditus), Paul used more succinct words like *brother, fellow worker, fellow soldier,* and *messenger.* You don't earn eulogies like these from appearing at an occasional youth rally or showing up at church picnics. These are compliments earned over years and tears . . . Epaphroditus. The only thing longer than his name was his staying power.

Re-liable. *Liable* means responsible. *Re* means over and over again.

I'm wondering if this study has found its way into the hands of some contemporary saints of reliability. If such is the case . . . thank you.

Thank you, senior saints, for a generation of prayer and forest clearing.

Thank you, teachers, for the countless Sunday school lessons, prepared and delivered with tenderness.

Thank you, missionaries, for your bravery in sharing the timeless truth in a foreign tongue.

Thank you, preachers. You thought we weren't listening, but we were. And your stubborn sowing of God's seed is bearing fruit you may never see this side of the great harvest.

Thanks to all of you who practice on Monday what you hear on Sunday. You spent selfless hours with orphans, at keyboards, in board meetings, on knees, in hospital wards, away from families, and on assembly lines. It is upon the back of your fidelity that the gospel rides. (From *God Came Near* by Max Lucado.)

REACTION

7. Who are the specific Christians who, humanly speaking, are responsible for your spiritual life and growth?

_____

_____

_____

_____

8. How can you show your gratitude to your spiritual leaders and mentors?

9. How are modern-day small groups similar to ancient house churches?

10. Epaphras wrestled in prayer for the believers in Colossae. What are your prayer habits—specifically your habits of praying for other believers?

11. Who needs your encouragement in a fashion similar to the exhortation Paul gave Archippus?

12. Contrast Acts 15:37–40 and Colossians 4:10 with Colossians 4:14 and 2 Timothy 4:10. How do the opposite life trajectories of Mark and Demas sober you?

_____

_____

_____

_____

_____

_____

_____

LIFE LESSONS

At the end of this Christ-centered, theology-drenched letter, Paul concludes with an endearing snapshot of community. Aristarchus, Mark, Justus, Epaphras, Luke, Demas, Nympha, Archippus . . . ordinary folks serving an extraordinary God in a myriad of ways. The passage is permeated with affection and punctuated with purpose. All alone, these individuals would not have much of an impact. But ministering together, they helped turn the first-century world "upside down" (Acts 17:6 NKJV). This is God's design for the Christian life—uniquely gifted people banding together to accomplish his kingdom plan. Resist the modern trends toward individualism and personal autonomy. Link up with other believers to grow and serve.

DEVOTION

Father, thank you for the brief but profound reminder in this passage that in calling us to yourself, you have also called us to one another. Increase our hunger for and commitment to our community of spiritual brothers and sisters.

JOURNALING

How is your spiritual community better because of your devotion to it? How is your life better because of your spiritual community's investment in you?

FOR FURTHER READING

To complete the books of Colossians and Philemon during this twelve-part study, read Colossians 4:7–18. For more Bible passages on spiritual community, read John 13:34–35; Acts 2:42–47; Romans 12:3–16; 1 Corinthians 12; Galatians 6:1–10; and Ephesians 4:1–16.

THE MIRACLE OF FORGIVENESS

*So if you consider me a partner, welcome him as
you would welcome me. If he has done you any
wrong or owes you anything, charge it to me.*
PHILEMON 1:17–18

REFLECTION

Think back over your childhood, especially your adolescent years. What were one or two of your most regrettable choices or hurtful actions that you made? More importantly, how did those you hurt treat you after the fact?

SITUATION

The letter of Philemon is linked to Colossians in that the recipients were all located in the same city of Colossae. However, while Colossians is a letter of instruction to a community of believers, Philemon is directed to a particular person in that community. In the letter, Paul makes a personal plea on behalf of Onesimus, a slave from Colossae who stole from his master, Philemon, and fled from him. Paul led him to faith in Christ, and now he is sending Onesimus back to his master with this letter that encourages mercy, forgiveness, and Christian love.

OBSERVATION

Read Philemon 1:1–21 from the New International
Version or the New King James Version.

NEW INTERNATIONAL VERSION

[1] Paul, a prisoner of Christ Jesus, and Timothy our brother,

To Philemon our dear friend and fellow worker—[2] also to Apphia our sister and Archippus our fellow soldier—and to the church that meets in your home:

[3] Grace and peace to you from God our Father and the Lord Jesus Christ.

[4] I always thank my God as I remember you in my prayers, [5] because I hear about your love for all his holy people and your faith in the Lord Jesus. [6] I pray that your partnership with us in the faith may be effective in deepening your understanding of every good thing we share for the sake of Christ. [7] Your love has given me great joy and encouragement, because you, brother, have refreshed the hearts of the Lord's people.

[8] Therefore, although in Christ I could be bold and order you to do what you ought to do, [9] yet I prefer to appeal to you on the basis of love. It is as none other than Paul—an old man and now also a prisoner of Christ Jesus— [10] that I appeal to you for my son Onesimus, who became my son while I was in chains. [11] Formerly he was useless to you, but now he has become useful both to you and to me.

[12] I am sending him—who is my very heart—back to you. [13] I would have liked to keep him with me so that he could take your place in helping me while I am in chains for the gospel.[14] But I did not want to do anything without your consent, so that any favor you do would not seem forced but would be voluntary. [15] Perhaps the reason he was separated from you for a little while was that you might have him back forever— [16] no longer as a slave, but better than a slave, as a dear brother. He is very dear to me but even dearer to you, both as a fellow man and as a brother in the Lord.

¹⁷ So if you consider me a partner, welcome him as you would welcome me. ¹⁸ If he has done you any wrong or owes you anything, charge it to me. ¹⁹ I, Paul, am writing this with my own hand. I will pay it back—not to mention that you owe me your very self. ²⁰ I do wish, brother, that I may have some benefit from you in the Lord; refresh my heart in Christ. ²¹ Confident of your obedience, I write to you, knowing that you will do even more than I ask.

NEW KING JAMES VERSION

¹ Paul, a prisoner of Christ Jesus, and Timothy our brother,

To Philemon our beloved friend and fellow laborer, ² to the beloved Apphia, Archippus our fellow soldier, and to the church in your house:

³ Grace to you and peace from God our Father and the Lord Jesus Christ.

⁴ I thank my God, making mention of you always in my prayers, ⁵ hearing of your love and faith which you have toward the Lord Jesus and toward all the saints, ⁶ that the sharing of your faith may become effective by the acknowledgment of every good thing which is in you in Christ Jesus. ⁷ For we have great joy and consolation in your love, because the hearts of the saints have been refreshed by you, brother.

⁸ Therefore, though I might be very bold in Christ to command you what is fitting, ⁹ yet for love's sake I rather appeal to you—being such a one as Paul, the aged, and now also a prisoner of Jesus Christ—¹⁰ I appeal to you for my son Onesimus, whom I have begotten while in my chains, ¹¹ who once was unprofitable to you, but now is profitable to you and to me.

¹² I am sending him back. You therefore receive him, that is, my own heart, ¹³ whom I wished to keep with me, that on your behalf he might minister to me in my chains for the gospel. ¹⁴ But without your consent I wanted to do nothing, that your good deed might not be by compulsion, as it were, but voluntary.

¹⁵ For perhaps he departed for a while for this purpose, that you might receive him forever, ¹⁶ no longer as a slave but more than a slave—a

beloved brother, especially to me but how much more to you, both in the flesh and in the Lord.

[17] If then you count me as a partner, receive him as you would me. [18] But if he has wronged you or owes anything, put that on my account. [19] I, Paul, am writing with my own hand. I will repay—not to mention to you that you owe me even your own self besides. [20] Yes, brother, let me have joy from you in the Lord; refresh my heart in the Lord.

[21] Having confidence in your obedience, I write to you, knowing that you will do even more than I say.

EXPLORATION

1. In Paul's day, it was the wives who held the day-to-day responsibilities of the slaves in the household. Why is this fact significant when you consider that Paul included her in his greeting?

_____

_____

_____

2. Onesimus was a thief who eventually became Paul's "very heart" (verse 12). How can you account for such a change? How do you think Philemon would have responded to these words?

_____

_____

_____

3. What lessons on respect do you see in this postcard of an epistle?

_____

_____

_____

4. What reasons does Paul give for why Philemon was "separated" from Onesimus for a time? How might this have compelled Philemon to take him back?

_____

_____

_____

_____

_____

5. Some might argue that the situation between Onesimus and Philemon was none of Paul's business. Paul obviously felt otherwise. What are the implications of this for you?

_____

_____

_____

_____

6. When, if ever, do you think it appropriate for a Christian leader like Paul to "pull rank" on another Christian? What situations would warrant this response?

_____

_____

_____

_____

INSPIRATION

The merciful, says Jesus, are shown mercy. They witness grace. They are blessed because they are testimonies to a greater goodness. Forgiving others allows us to see how God has forgiven us. The dynamic of giving grace is the key to understanding grace, for it is when we forgive others that we begin to feel what God feels.

Jesus told the story of a king who decided to close out all his accounts with those who worked for him (see Matthew 18:21–35). He called in his debtors and told them to pay. One man owed an amount too great to return—a debt that could never be repaid. But when the king saw the man and heard his story, his heart went out to him, and he erased the debt.

As the man was leaving the palace grounds, he encountered a fellow employee who owed him a small sum. He grabbed the debtor and choked him, demanding payment. When the fellow begged for mercy, no mercy was granted. Instead, the one who had just been forgiven had his debtor thrown into jail. When word of this got to the king, he became livid. And Jesus says, "In anger his master turned him over to the jailers to be tortured, until he should pay back all he owed" (Matthew 18:34).

Could someone actually be forgiven a debt of millions and be unable to forgive a debt of hundreds? Could a person be set free and then imprison another?

You don't have to be a theologian to answer those questions; you only have to look in the mirror. Who among us has not begged God for mercy on Sunday and then demanded justice on Monday? Who hasn't served as a bottleneck instead of a conduit of God's love? Is there anyone who doesn't, at one time or the other, "show contempt for the riches of his [God's] kindness, tolerance and patience, not realizing that God's kindness leads you towards repentance" (Romans 2:4)?

Notice what God does when we calibrate our compassion. He turns us over to be tortured. Tortured by anger. Choked by bitterness. Consumed by revenge. Such is the punishment for one who tastes God's grace but refuses to share it.

But for the one who tastes God's grace and then gives it to others, the reward is a blessed liberation. The prison door is thrown open, and the prisoner set free is yourself. (From *The Applause of Heaven* by Max Lucado.)

REACTION

7. When have you been most amazed and moved by God's mercy?

_____

_____

_____

_____

_____

_____

8. What are the risks of seeking forgiveness? What are the risks of _not_ seeking it?

_____

_____

_____

_____

_____

_____

9. What are the dangers of forgiving one who has betrayed you?

_____

_____

_____

_____

_____

_____

10. When does anger become unforgiveness? When does unforgiveness become bitterness?

_____

_____

_____

_____

_____

11. At some point, Paul obviously suggested that Onesimus go back to his master. What do you think was said? How do you think Onesimus responded to the idea?

_____

_____

_____

_____

12. In what relationship might God be leading you to serve as a peacemaker this week?

_____

_____

_____

_____

LIFE LESSONS

What do we do when someone slights us, rebuffs us, or intentionally hurts us? We always have a choice, you know. We can relive that affront over and over, slowly building a wall of resentment and bitterness around our hearts. Regrettably, lots of people do that. Or we can, by God's grace and in his strength, elect to show supernatural mercy. Despite our wounds, and irrespective of our feelings, we _can_ make the choice to forgive. What exactly is forgiveness? It is canceling the moral and personal debt another person now owes us because of his or her failure to treat us with love and respect. When we forgive, we give our offenders and the world a peek at God's heart. And we ensure that our own hearts don't become hardened.

DEVOTION

Father, forgive us for holding a grudge against others. In the same way you have forgiven us, we want to forgive them. Help us to learn the beautiful and rare skill of showing mercy. Remind us daily of the promise, "Blessed are the merciful, for they will be shown mercy."

JOURNALING

What steps will you take today to forgive those who have offended you— even if they have not yet made the effort to reach out to you to request it?

_____

_____

_____

_____

_____

_____

_____

_____

_____

_____

FOR FURTHER READING

To complete the books of Colossians and Philemon during this twelve-part study, read Philemon 1:1–25. For more Bible passages on forgiveness, read Micah 6:8; Matthew 5:7; Mark 11:25; Luke 6:36; 17:3–4; Ephesians 4:32; Colossians 3:13; and James 2:13.

LEADER'S GUIDE FOR SMALL GROUPS

Thank you for your willingness to lead a group through *Life Lessons from Colossians and Philemon*. The rewards of being a leader are different from those of participating, and we hope you find your own walk with Jesus deepened by this experience. During the twelve lessons in this study, you will guide your group through selected passages in Colossians and Philemon and explore the key themes of the letter. There are several elements in this leader's guide that will help you as you structure your study and reflection time, so be sure to follow along and take advantage of each one.

BEFORE YOU BEGIN

Before your first meeting, make sure the group members have their own copy of the *Life Lessons from Colossians and Philemon* study guide so they can follow along and have their answers written out ahead of time. Alternately, you can hand out the guides at your first meeting and give the group some time to look over the material and ask any preliminary questions. Be sure to send a sheet around the room during that first meeting and have the members write down their name, phone number, and email address so you can keep in touch with them during the week.

There are two ways to structure the duration of the study. You can choose to cover each lesson individually for a total of twelve weeks of discussion, or you can combine two lessons together per week for a total of six weeks of discussion. (Note that if the group members read the selected passages of Scripture for each lesson, they will cover the entire books of Colossians and Philemon during the study.) The following table illustrates these options:

Twelve-Week Format

Week	Lessons Covered	Reading
1	Faith, Hope, and Love	Colossians 1:1–8
2	Praying with Power	Colossians 1:9–14
3	The Supremacy of Christ	Colossians 1:15–23
4	Serving Christ	Colossians 1:24–29
5	Walking with Christ	Colossians 2:1–10
6	Foolish Philosophies	Colossians 2:11–23
7	Living Differently	Colossians 3:1–17
8	Home, Sweet Home	Colossians 3:18–21
9	What About Work?	Colossians 3:22–4:1
10	A Mouth That Makes a Difference	Colossians 4:2–6
11	Companions on the Journey	Colossians 4:7–18
12	The Miracle of Forgiveness	Philemon 1–21

Six-Week Format

Week	Lessons Covered	Reading
1	Faith, Hope, and Love / Praying with Power	Colossians 1:1–14
2	The Supremacy of Christ / Serving Christ	Colossians 1:15–29
3	Walking with Christ / Foolish Philosophies	Colossians 2:1–23
4	Living Differently / Home, Sweet Home	Colossians 3:1–21
5	What About Work? / A Mouth That Makes a Difference	Colossians 3:22–4:6
6	Companions on the Journey / The Miracle of Forgiveness	Colossians 4:7–18; Philemon 1–21

Generally, the ideal size you will want for the group is between eight to ten people, which ensures everyone will have enough time to participate in discussions. If you have more people, you might want to break up the main group into smaller subgroups. Encourage those who show up at the first meeting to commit to attending the duration of the study, as this will help the group members get to know each other, create stability for the group, and help you know how to prepare each week.

Each of the lessons begins with a brief reflection that highlights the theme you will be discussing that week. As you begin your group time, have the group members briefly respond to the opening question to get them thinking about the topic at hand. Some people may want to tell a long story in response to one of these questions, but the goal is to keep the answers brief. Ideally, you want everyone in the group to get a chance to answer, so try to keep the responses to just a few minutes. If you have more talkative group members, say up front that everyone needs to limit his or her answer to two minutes.

Give the group members a chance to answer, but tell them to feel free to pass if they wish. With the rest of the study, it's generally not a good idea to have everyone answer every question—a free-flowing discussion is more desirable. But with the opening reflection question, you can go around the circle. Encourage shy people to share, but don't force them.

Before your first meeting, let the group members know how the lessons are broken down. During your group discussion time the members will be drawing on the answers they wrote to the Exploration and Reaction sections, so encourage them to always complete these ahead of time. Also, invite them to bring any questions and insights they uncovered while reading to your next meeting, especially if they had a breakthrough moment or if they didn't understand something they read.

WEEKLY PREPARATION

As the leader, there are a few things you should do to prepare for each meeting:

- *Read through the lesson.* This will help you to become familiar with the content and know how to structure the discussion times.
- *Decide which questions you want to discuss.* Depending on how you structure your group time, you may not be able to cover every

question. So select the questions ahead of time that you absolutely want the group to explore.

- *Be familiar with the questions you want to discuss.* When the group meets you'll be watching the clock, so you want to make sure you are familiar with the Bible study questions you have selected. You can then spend time in the passage again when the group meets. In this way, you'll ensure you have the passage more deeply in your mind than your group members.

- *Pray for your group.* Pray for your group members throughout the week and ask God to lead them as they study his Word.

- *Bring extra supplies to your meeting.* The members should bring their own pens for writing notes, but it's a good idea to have extras available for those who forget. You may also want to bring paper and additional Bibles.

Note that in many cases there will not be one "right" answer to the question. Answers will vary, especially when the group members are being asked to share their personal experiences.

STRUCTURING THE DISCUSSION TIME

You will need to determine with your group how long you want to meet each week so you can plan your time accordingly. Generally, most groups like to meet for either sixty minutes or ninety minutes, so you could use one of the following schedules:

Section	60 Minutes	90 Minutes
WELCOME (members arrive and get settled)	5 minutes	10 minutes
REFLECTION (discuss the opening question for the lesson)	10 minutes	15 minutes
DISCUSSION (discuss the Bible study questions in the Exploration and Reaction sections)	35 minutes	50 minutes
PRAYER/CLOSING (pray together as a group and dismiss)	10 minutes	15 minutes

As the group leader, it is up to you to keep track of the time and keep things moving along according to your schedule. You might want to set a timer for each segment so both you and the group members know when your time is up. (Note that there are some good phone apps for timers that play a gentle chime or other pleasant sound instead of a disruptive noise.) Don't feel pressured to cover every question you have selected if the group has a good discussion going. Again, it's not necessary to go around the circle and make everyone share.

Don't be concerned if the group members are silent or slow to share. People are often quiet when they are pulling together their ideas, and this might be a new experience for them. Just ask a question and let it hang in the air until someone shares. You can then say, "Thank you. What about others? What came to you when you reflected on the passage?"

GROUP DYNAMICS

Leading a group through *Life Lessons from Colossians and Philemon* will prove to be highly rewarding both to you and your group members—but that doesn't mean you will not encounter any challenges along the way! Discussions can get off track. Group members may not be sensitive to the needs and ideas of others. Some might worry they will be expected to talk about matters that make them feel awkward. Others may express comments that result in disagreements. To help ease this strain on you and the group, consider the following ground rules:

- When someone raises a question or comment that is off the main topic, suggest you deal with it another time, or, if you feel led to go in that direction, let the group know you will be spending some time discussing it.
- If someone asks a question you don't know how to answer, admit it and move on. At your discretion, feel free to invite group members to comment on questions that call for personal experience.

- If you find one or two people are dominating the discussion time, direct a few questions to others in the group. Outside the main group time, ask the more dominating members to help you draw out the quieter ones. Work to make them a part of the solution instead of the problem.
- When a disagreement occurs, encourage the group members to process the matter in love. Encourage those on opposite sides to restate what they heard the other side say about the matter, and then invite each side to evaluate if that perception is accurate. Lead the group in examining other Scriptures related to the topic and look for common ground.

When any of these issues arise, encourage your group members to follow the words from the Bible: "Love one another" (John 13:34), "If it is possible, as far as it depends on you, live at peace with everyone" (Romans 12:18), and, "Be quick to listen, slow to speak and slow to become angry" (James 1:19).

Thank you again for taking the time to lead your group. May God reward your efforts and dedication and make your time together in this study fruitful for his kingdom.

ALSO AVAILABLE IN THE LIFE LESSONS SERIES

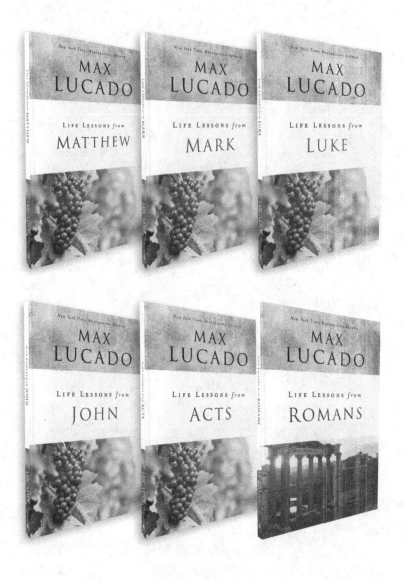

Now available wherever books and ebooks are sold.